Planting Churches that Reproduce

Starting a Network of Simple Churches

Joel Comiskey

Published By CCS Publishing

CCS Publishing

www.joelcomiskeygroup.com

Published by CCS Publishing
23890 Brittlebush Circle
Moreno Valley, CA 92557 USA
1-888-344-CELL

Cover design by Josh Talbot
Editing by Scott Boren
Copy editing by Susan Osborn and Brian McClemore

All Scripture quotations, unless otherwise indicated, are from the Holy Bible, New International Version, Copyright ©1973, 1978, 1984 by International Bible Society. Used by permission.

CCS Publishing is the book-publishing division of Joel Comiskey Group, a resource and coaching ministry dedicated to equipping leaders for cell-based ministry.

Find us on the World Wide Web at **www.joelcomiskeygroup.com**

Publisher's Cataloging-in-Publication

Comiskey, Joel, 1956-

     Planting churches that reproduce : starting a network
  of simple churches / by Joel Comiskey.

     p. cm.

     Includes bibliographical references and index.

     LCCN 2007909331

     ISBN-13: 9780979067969

     ISBN-10: 0979067960

     1. Church development, New. 2. Church growth.

    3. Cell churches.   I. Title.

    BV652.24.C66 2008   254'.1

Praise for *Planting Churches that Reproduce*

"There is an old saying, 'Better late than never, but best never late.' Where has this book been? How different might the church be today if Comiskey's invaluable resource had been available even ten years ago? Don't discover Comiskey ten years from now and exclaim, 'Where have I been!' The book we've needed and been waiting for is here now. Tag, you're it."
— **LEONARD SWEET** Drew University, George Fox Evangelical Seminary, sermons.com

"Here is a thoroughly practical, encouraging, and thoughtful contribution to the small but growing body of literature on multiplication movements. This is an important book not only because it involves a return to a more genuinely biblical ecclesiology, but also because it envisions the much more dynamic form of church that will advance the cause of Jesus in the 21st Century."
— **ALAN HIRSCH** Author of The Forgotten Ways and The Shaping of Things to Come, Co-founder of shapevine.com

"Joel Comiskey brings both his experience and the experience of others together in a clear, easy to understand fashion that will be helpful to any simple church planter today. As I read, I kept thinking of chapters I wanted to recommend to the various church planters I coach. Based on timeless principles of church planting, Comiskey lays a firm foundation for multiplying churches which I believe is on the heart of God. His practical application of these principles keeps the reader focused on the path toward church planting success."
— **JEANNETTE BULLER** Church planter and coach

"Joel Comiskey does a great job in his book of explaining what a simple church is and how to plant them. He provides solid theology, numerous examples, and strategic steps for planting simple churches. We will use it with our planters as a resource. I've read a lot of books on simple, cell, house churches defending them or promoting them - I don't think I've read anything as clear and as concise as this or as practical to get them started as this."
— **BOB ROBERTS** Pastor NorthWood, author Transformation, Glocalization, The Multiplying Church

"Joel Comiskey's lifelong passion for multiplying churches does not allow him to get stuck in the past. I love this excellent book because it is a book for the future. Joel's blueprint will help many find their proper position for enriching their life and for extending the kingdom of God."
— **PETER WAGNER** Presiding Apostle, International Coalition of Apostles

Praise for *Planting Churches that Reproduce*

"Joel Comiskey is a veteran church planter. His new book "Planting Churches that Reproduce" is biblical, practical and inspirational. If indeed church planters are going to get serious about evangelistic reproducing movements that start new testament churches then we must take a long and creative look at Simple churches or some variation of the house church movement. The typical suburban church planting model will not get the job done alone."
— **DR. TOM JONES** Author, Stadia East Regional Director, professor, and veteran church planter

"Over the last ten years Joel's writings and research have deeply influenced who we are as a people. His genuine love for Jesus and his heart to capture what God is doing and saying is bearing great fruit for the body of Christ. His latest book, *Planting Churches that Reproduce,* is at the heart of what God is speaking to the body of Christ worldwide, whether in the United States or around the world."
— **JIMMY SEIBERT** Senior pastor of Antioch Community Church

"Once again, Joel Comiskey has felt the pulse of the body of Christ and has given a prescription for its well being. This book is a combination of spiritual insights coupled with personal experience in the field of planting Biblical communities. I recommend this for the group that God forms to form a new Christ centered missional congregation."
— **RALPH NEIGHBOUR** Author, professor, and church planter

"Planting Churches that Reproduce is a good solid manual for planters who want to get back to the basics and discover what church is really all about. Comiskey helps Christian leaders make the paradigm shift from buildings and events to people and evangelism--and then provides clear strategies for moving forward. He underscores that what makes a church effective is not about size so much as it is about how well it can reproduce."
— **BOB LOGAN** Author, professor, and church planter

"Planting Churches that Reproduce is an important piece in the body of work God has produced through Joel Comiskey. This book builds upon Joel's extensive research, personal experiences and previous books. It takes us back to simplicity: the simple church and the simple steps for planting that simple church. But Joel also shows us how God forms the basic simple church into larger sizes and shapes that are appropriate for the 21st Century world."
— **BILL BECKHAM** Church planter and author of numerous books

Praise for *Planting Churches that Reproduce*

"Joel Comiskey's latest book, Planting Churches that Reproduce, is an easy-to-read, inspiring, educational, and practical nuts-and-bolts tool to help church planters and church plants of any style get to where God is asking them to go. There is a twist that is worth the price of the book. Comiskey examines the growing global phenomenon of 'simple church networks' which challenges conventional assumptions and complicated models of what it means to be an effective Great Commission church. Simple, strategic, and scriptural are the watchwords for the church in this hour."
— **RAD ZDERO, PhD** Author of *The Global House Church Movement*, Editor of *Nexus: The World House Church Movement Reader*

"In the late twentieth century there was only one or two books on church planting. So I wrote my book-*Planting Growing Churches*, because America desperately needed more churches that would reach unchurched Baby Boomers.

However, eight years into the twenty-first century, we have a number of books that will guide us not only in starting churches to reach the Boomers but for the Next Generation. Joel Comiskey's *Planting Churches that Reproduce* is one of these books. If you're a church planter or part of a church plant that is passionate about reaching the Next Generation-the future of the North American church, then this book is a must read!"
— **AUBREY MALPHURS** Lead Vision Navigator with the Malphurs Group, Senior Professor at Dallas Seminary

"In *Planting Churches that Reproduce* Joel paints pictures of multiplying churches from real life examples. He uses research, reflection on biblical principles and field tested strategies to show how struggle and space are critical to developing healthy multiplying churches. Joel applies simple biblical principles to a variety of models from cell churches to house church networks to stand alone house churches. As he describes real life examples of each model he offers wise critique and a clear practical focus on prayer and building relational webs. Could church really be as simple as Christ followers gathering in a home supporting a life style of loving God and others? This is a book every church leader should read to more effectively align with Christ's work of building His church."
— **DR. ROY KING** Professor of Leadership of Columbia International University

Praise for *Planting Churches that Reproduce*

"*Planting Churches That Reproduce* is yet another great resource from Joel Comiskey. In this useful tool, full of practical application and case studies, Joel draws from the years of actual experience now under the belt of the cell-church movement, to demystify and simplify the church planting process. This clearly written and inspiring manual is a breath of fresh hope for the weary saints of God hungry for the harvest. A recommended must read for all cell-celebration leaders and leaders-in-development."
— **SUSAN M. SKOMMESA** Lead Pastor, Verdugo Community Free Methodist Church, Superintendent for FMC in Urban LA

"I highly recommend Joel's new book "Planting Churches that Reproduce!" This insightful book is not just about theory. It is filled with field tested examples of healthy new churches being planted, and provides practical spiritual insights and principles for us to learn and emulate. Planting simple churches that network together is vital to fulfilling our Lord's Great Commission. This book will serve as a practical manual to help us on this journey."
— **LARRY KREIDER** International Director, Dove Chrisitan Fellowship Intl.

"Joel Comiskey is one of those rare church thinkers who understands how cell groups form the basis for an organic, simple and growing church. In this book he describes a clear step-by-step process for birthing evangelistic churches that are built upon cell groups. I have often said that two of the most common missing ingredients in churches are the lack of expansive prayer and the lack of expansive cell groups. Every church leader who wants to recapture the organic, simple and life-changing nature of the church will discover in this book a roadmap for church change: into something more simple, connected and healthy."
— **BOB WHITESEL** McGavran Award winner for Outstanding Leadership in Church Growth and author of five books

"Joel Comiskeys' books have always been a blessing to me personally—they have brought special insight into issues that people in cell churches are interested in. 'Joel, you have out done yourself again! You have written a book that will be used to bring the house church and cell church people together. Well done!' All those who are interested in the new move of God for these final days must read this book!"
— **BEN WONG** Advisory pastor of Shepherd Community Grace Church, founder of CCMN

Table of Contents

Table of Contents

Acknowledgements

This book has taken years to research, write, edit, perfect, edit, perfect, edit . . .and finally see light. In the long process, many hands and eyes have handled and contributed to the final work. Several people deserve special recognition.

I want to thank Steve and Linda Cordle for taking the time to edit this book. Jay Stanwood offered incredible insight into how to clarify obscure phrases. John and Mary Reith, as always, offered lots of encouragement and keen insight. Oliver Lutz carefully critiqued the book. I appreciated his objective analysis. I want to thank Patricia Barrett for her helpful suggestions and practical advice.

Rad Zdero went way beyond the call of duty to give me deep insight into the house church movement and the biblical text.

Kelly Bokovay spent lots of time on the manuscript. Kelly's church planting experience made his critique very valuable.

Rae Holt offered me key, foundational advice. He was also a great source of encouragement.

My good friend Rob Campbell took precious time reading this manuscript and helped steer me away from some dangerous landmines.

I appreciated Brad Briscoe's practical advice on what he liked and didn't like about the manuscript.

Anne White thoroughly critiqued this manuscript, even scouring the endnotes for mistakes and errors. Her insights were invaluable to the final draft of this book.

I really appreciated Brian McClemore's helpful criticism about the weaknesses of my church planting arguments and how to improve the overall book. He spent a lot of time critiquing this book, and the book is much better as a result of his hard work.

I appreciated Susan Osborn's expertise in copy-editing the final edition of this book.

Scott Boren, my chief editor, continues to do an incredible editing job. We've been together on nineteen of my twenty-one books.

I also thank God for my wonderful wife, Celyce, for the listening ear and solid counsel she's given me throughout the process of writing this book.

Foreword

I planted my first church in 1988 among the urban poor in Buffalo, NY. At the time, I was aware of only one book on church planting. Church planting conferences didn't exist; neither did church planting websites, webcasts, or blogs. Outside of a call to plant and a radical faith in the Lord of the Harvest, church planters were largely void of any sort of information base from which to glean in those days.

Now everything has changed. It seems like new church planting resources (e.g., conferences, books, blogs, webcasts, podcasts, and websites) are constantly popping up. And, as Martha Stewart would say, "It is a good thing." These new resources provide tools to help church planters in a new way.

Successful church planters are life-long learners. Learners are gleaners and processors of information. Successful church planters thrive off of conversations with other planters, books by church planters, and conferences led by church planters. Even after planting several churches, I'm still a learner. If I ever stop learning, I lose my focus. The same is true for you.

I know, maybe you are thinking, "but I mostly learn from my personal experiences." Or maybe you are a doer and you learn from doing. Sure, personal experiences lend much towards personal growth. But what if you could add to your own knowledge by learning from someone else's personal experiences, from their mistakes and from their successes? Now we're talking. This is why I'm glad you've joined me in reading Joel Comiskey's newest book, *Planting Churches that Reproduce*.

If you are like me, you have been tweaked as you interacted with professors, authors, conference speakers, or denominational officials trying to teach about church planting without having actually planted themselves. I am sure they mean well and in many cases know a few things about planting—but it sounds a bit like "do as I say, not as I do." They're experts who tell you everything you're doing wrong in church planting, even though they've never planted a church. Unlike these well meaning givers of theoretical advice, Joel is a voice to be heard. He is a church planter. He's been in the trenches. He knows what it's like to experience both the hurts and the joys of church planting.

Joel has walked a long mile in the church planter's shoes. Along the journey, Joel has learned the things he now shares with you, not only from his own experiences, but also by his extensive networking with church planters across North America and all the way to South America, Africa, India, China, and beyond.

In this, his newest book, Joel has given us a valuable tool in relating the principles of Jesus' earthly ministry and of the rapid growth in the early New Testament church to the need to create and network reproducing simple churches.

Church planters can be some of the most amazing people in ministry today. Many have followed God's call into church planting at great cost. Some have left high paying positions with established churches while others have left promising careers in the corporate world, trusting God for their every need, as they seek to put the needs of the unchurched before their very own.

Church planting can run the gamut, from well-funded planters launching mega churches with mega bucks, to planters with more faith than cents, pursuing a call and a dream to be a part of something that only God could orchestrate. If we are going to truly impact the growing lostness in North America and throughout the world, we must recognize not only the value of the church planters who've been blessed to launch big, but we must also recognize the importance of planting churches without great resources and fanfare.

God Uses Little Things to Make a Great Impact

The history of God's activity in the hearts of mankind is replete with examples of God's use of ordinary people with ordinary means to do extraordinary things. God used the common harlot, Rahab, to spare the Israelite spies as they scoped out Jericho in the land of

Canaan. God used little David to kill a mighty giant of a man and a fierce invading army with a little pebble and a sling.

God has used ordinary men and women, many without their own copy of the Bible, to launch church planting movements in difficult places like China. The success of the rapidly growing church in China isn't because of money. As I'm sure you know, the Chinese government isn't exactly kind to Christians and certainly not to the underground church. Yet, the underground Chinese Church is growing exponentially through the teaching of the Gospel in rapidly multiplying house churches. It's a simple model being propagated by everyday, ordinary people, many of which are new believers. What can we learn from how God is working and moving there?

If we are going to see a church planting movement in North America, it most likely will not come from the mega churches in affluent suburbs—as good and important as those are. Most planters simply will not have the money for all the flashy bells and whistles to create marketing systems and concert-like sound and lighting effects used by the big boys. Yet, the "rest of us" are not insignificant, and the potential scope of their impact doesn't have to be limited because of fewer funds and limited partnerships. If we are to see a church planting movement in North America, as we have in other parts of the world, it will come from ordinary people becoming missional and incarnational church planters, embracing the unchurched culture through simple, reproducible churches that won't necessarily rely on big budgets and big buildings.

Don't get me wrong, I'm not opposed to big budgets for church planters. God has greatly used many church plants that were blessed to launch big (I've launched one myself). God is even greatly using many established churches that have grown to mega church status over the course of time. Yet God has used even more of our average, ordinary church plants, who've started with much less, to make a far greater impact on the lostness of our continent and world.

Cell Churches & House Churches Are Readily Reproducible

Joel Comiskey has given us a glimpse into a growing cell church movement through his previous books, *The Church that Multiplies* and *Reap the Harvest*. In still another book, *Leadership Explosion*, Joel has helped us to understand leadership principles for identifying and training leaders who will identify and train other leaders in an ongoing effort to begin more mission outposts for the proclamation of the Gospel. Now with this, his latest book, Joel has enriched our understanding in the creation and growth of a reproducible model for church planting through simple cell churches and networks of house churches.

Not everyone will have a bank roll of $100,000 start a church. But everyone can start small and full of faith, by investing in one person and then in a small group of people who can be trained to reach others. I believe one of our greatest needs is for a simple, reproducible model for starting many new and multiplying churches.

This book challenges us to reconsider a common church planting model from the 1980's forward where massive resources have been poured into launch efforts to take a new church from 20 to 300 in the space of one service. I have used this approach several times and it worked. It still works today. However, I have also seen this approach bomb. Sometimes no one came. Other times, great crowds came out to a well-advertised launch service but then got lost in the shuffle because the church plant's leadership wasn't trained and ready to handle the influx of new people from a huge launch service. Launching is often a tool God uses—but there are other ways where a church may grow more naturally. It goes without saying, as we look at the early church, the church largely grew in a more natural way. Sure, there were accounts of huge days like the Day of Pentecost, but by and far as the New Testament Church spread and took root, it was planted person by person as one person invested in the life of another who invested in the life of another.

The early church was catapulted to growth as the Spirit of God used the proclamation of the message of Christ by believers who just couldn't keep quiet about Jesus. While appearing before the Sanhedrin, Peter and John preached to their captors, risking great punishment, even death, saying "for we are unable to stop speaking about what we have seen and heard" (Acts 4:20, Holman Christian Standard Bible). They invested in others, who invested in others, and the church grew and grew. They simply couldn't keep silent, because they'd seen the Savior. As the message spread and as the early church grew, many were added to the number who had never seen Jesus face to face, but they too had been changed by Christ's words as they were spread, person to person and from town to town.

In this book, Joel highlights the benefits of the simple models of churches that can rapidly expand through cell or house church networks. His insights on reproducing churches will encourage those engaged in church planting to consider the benefits of moving from a call and a vision to the creation of small groups where leaders can be identified and trained, so that they might create and lead new small groups that will continue multiplying into more leaders and more small groups. Eventually the multiplication of small groups and leaders could lead the church planter to move the church to begin holding regular worship gatherings where all the small groups or house churches would join together for celebration. The ultimate goal of this new faith community would be to impact still more unchurched communities through the multiplication of the small groups into the creation of other new churches which would continue the whole process until Christ returns for his bride.

Grounded in Experience, Holding Forth God's Word

Comiskey's approach isn't theoretical. As he lays out in this book, thousands of simple churches are multiplying all over the world and, increasingly, here in North America we are seeing this simple church philosophy multiply into the creation of an expanding base of cell churches that, I believe, could greatly impact the lostness throughout major cities across North America.

Even if you are not called to lead in a cell church or house church context, you will find a set of transferable principles laid out in this book which will challenge and inspire you in the areas of small groups, leadership training, networking, evangelism, fund raising, and multiplication. Regardless of the model of church planting you have been called to, there are timeless lessons you can learn to assist you in your journey, and many of these principles are addressed in this book.

Perhaps one of the greatest benefits of this book is the way Joel links the Bible to real life in the church planting world. As Joel lays out in this book, the early New Testament Church looked radically different from most of today's North American churches.

I believe somewhere along the way we have become confused in thinking that it is our methods, marketing, programs, staff, and facilities that will grow the church. We've somehow forgotten the impact of God working through the Spirit of God to complete his intentions for the Word of God to serve as a catalyst for transforming lost sinners into becoming the redeemed people of God.

I'm sure that as you read Joel's words you will be challenged to lead your church or church plant to become more biblical in its approach to the lost and unchurched. What will that look like for you and your church? Though I can't know the specific details, I do know that the results of seeking to be more biblical in our approach to ministry will be far reaching as we seek to win the lost to faith in Jesus Christ.

Held by God's Hand

Finally, as fellow labors in the fields that are white and ready to be harvested, I would like to encourage you as Joel does. Church planting is tough. The church planter in Quebec may dream of an easier planting experience in Louisiana, while the church planter in Oregon may believe their journey would have been easier if only they were church planting in North Carolina or Texas. As one who has planted in New York, Pennsylvania, and now in Georgia, I can tell you from experience that church planting is hard work, anywhere. I've met with 1000's of church planters and pastors throughout the world who tell me the same.

Be faithful to the call God has given you. Preach the Word. Stay on your knees. Cherish your family. Love the people God has led you to reach and keep serving the King, Christ Jesus. Joel has some great comments about your King's desires for you and for those you seek to reach through church planting. As you read Joel's words, remember that you are not alone. Though there will be times you may feel abandoned and uncared for, hold to the God who is holding you. The babe in the manger who gave himself up for you on the Cross and rose again on day 3 is proof enough that God has his best plans in play for you.

Thanks Joel, for all that you continue to do for church planting and the growth of Christ's Kingdom.

Ed Stetzer, Ph.D.
Author, *Lost and Found* and *Planting Missional Churches*
www.newchurches.com

Introduction

Jim Montgomery, the founder of a church planting movement called DAWN, told about a meeting with Donald McGavran, the founder of the church growth movement. Montgomery writes:

> During the last months of Mary McGavran's illness, my wife Lyn would frequently spend time with her. Donald McGavran would be there, too, disregarding his own painful cancer while taking care of his beloved Mary. Lyn said to Donald McGavran, "You can be sure Jim and I will continue our commitment to church growth after you're gone,' McGavran snapped back, 'Don't call it church growth anymore, call it church multiplication! The only way we will get the job of the Great Commission done is to plant a church in every community in the world.[1]

Somewhere along the way, the church growth movement became associated with growing one church as large as possible. Donald McGavran perceived that problem and gave church growth a richer meaning: church multiplication.

Church multiplication is biblical. Jesus Christ Himself revealed a multiplication strategy when He raised up men and women who were willing to scatter and spread the seeds of faith all over the Roman Empire. They were willing to die for their beliefs in the face of incredible odds. These Christ followers planted churches to make new disciples and spread the faith.

To plant a church in every nation of the world requires a simple, reproducible strategy. It's not about growing a few churches larger and larger. Ori Brafman and Rod Beckstrom, in their book *The Starfish and the Spider*, point out that growing companies have a simple strategy that possesses the DNA of reproduction. If you cut off a starfish's leg, it grows a new one, and that leg can grow into an entirely new starfish. Decentralized, simple church planting operates like the starfish. It can grow and multiply any place in the world. It's not dependent on councils, committees, buildings, or money. Simple church planting offers the exciting possibility of new churches springing up everywhere. And indeed this is exactly what's happening all over the world.

In North America, there's been a flood of books promoting a simple understanding of the church of Jesus Christ. Neil Cole's book, *Organic Church;* George Barna's *Revolution;* and Thom Rainer's *Simple Church* all point to a yearning in the church today for simple structures that multiply. The question that various authors are trying to answer is, "How can we have a church planting movement in the twenty-first century?"

Church planting has been my life for the last twenty-five years. I started a church in downtown Long Beach, California from my home in 1983. In 1984, I listened to David Cho speak at Fuller Seminary. I was so impressed that I bought both his entire tape series and his new book and began to teach my leaders about the home group system. The church did grow and continues its ministry in downtown Long Beach to this day; as I look back, however, I now realize that God was primarily teaching me about simpler, more reproducible church planting strategies.

In 1994, four years into my first term as a missionary in Ecuador, we planted a church in Quito, Ecuador (along with a national lead pastor and another missionary couple). We took 150 people from the mother church, along with ten home groups. The church grew quickly and within six years had 280 cells and 1300 worshippers. My main role was guiding the small group infrastructure.

In September 2003, as a family we started a church in my home in Moreno Valley, CA called Wellspring. We multiplied the first home group many times and eventually gathered those groups together for celebration. I was the lead pastor for the first four and a half years. In June 2008, I became the church planting pastor of Wellspring, having turned the lead pastor role over to Eric Glover. Our goal from the beginning was to keep the church simple and reproducible—and for it to eventually become a church planting movement.

Church planting is not easy. Someone has said that it's like drinking from a fire hose—fast and furious. Throughout this book I hope to share the pain, struggles, and breakthroughs of my own church planting journey. More importantly, we'll look at biblical and practical principles that will help you, the church planter, lay a strong foundation to start simple, reproducible churches.

Section One

Simple Church Foundations

Planting Churches that Reproduce

Chapter One

Life in the Desert

In the summer of 2008, our family drove through the hot, dry desert of California and Arizona on our way to Colorado. I witnessed mile after mile of dry wasteland. At times I spotted an old sign that marked the failed attempt of a restaurant, gas station, or motel.

The desert has special meaning to me because I live in one. Moreno Valley, where I live, would be one of those run-down ghost towns if it weren't for the constant fight of humans to push back the desert realities.

In Moreno Valley, it's common for the temperature to soar to 105+ degrees. The hot, dry air not only affects people negatively, it does weird things to plant life. I've noticed every imaginable type of weed coming out of nowhere. Trying to keep real grass on my lawn takes persistent effort. Many homeowners have decided to just water the weeds, giving up trying to maintain real grass. Each fall, I've come to accept the fact that I'll have to replant entire swaths of grass. I've often compared my weed problem in Moreno Valley to Christ's church.

Churches also live in a hostile environment. The world, the flesh, and the devil pound against Christ's church, seeking to annihilate it. Without fresh leadership and evangelistic outreach, the natural tendency is stagnation, decline, and eventual death.

Church planting also keeps churches healthy and strong. Birthing new churches pushes back the encroaching desert and forms an oasis in the dryness. To stay healthy and fresh, churches need to plant churches that plant churches.

Plant or perish

God has blessed America with the gospel since the English Puritans emigrated in the early seventeenth century. Since those initial seeds, churches have blossomed, and many call America a Christian nation. The tendency of many is to think, "The church is already established in America. Why would we need to plant more churches?"

The fact is that Christianity is rapidly declining in America.

David Olson, a cutting edge researcher, wrote the book *The Crisis of the American Church* (2008). He used data of actual church attendance to show that 17.7% of the American population attended church on any given weekend in 2004 and that established churches showed zero percent growth. The one bright spot was church planting. Church plants added an increase of 7.8%. Olson explains that at no time in American history has the need for new churches been more critical. New church planters are needed now to scale back the decline and death of existing churches.[1] In order to survive, Christ's church must be replanted in every generation.

Whenever I minister in Europe, I see where America is headed: secularism gone astray and church buildings without the pulsating life of vibrant congregations. The story of the church in Europe over many centuries can best be understood as successive waves of ecclesiastical renewal, followed by periods of stagnation. Church planting movements were frequently the catalysts of renewal, but church planting was generally resisted by existing churches or regarded as extraordinary.[2]

When will a church be ready to plant a daughter? Most likely the church will never feel ready. The perception among most churches is that they're not big enough at their present size, no matter what it is. This same mindset affects the church in other areas as well. A church doesn't have quite enough finances to start a new church this year, so it decides to wait until next year or the year after. Decades later church planting becomes the great idea back then. The reality is that the ideal number of people and finances will always be perceived as being larger than what the church presently has.

Instead of waiting for that perfect day to arrive, churches need to change their priorities now! Multiplication is high on God's desire list—the multiplication of leaders, groups, and churches. The bursting forth of God's Spirit can't be contained. The Spirit often hovers over churches that convert intention into reality. One such example is Dove Christian Fellowship.

Larry Kreider never intended to start Dove Christian Fellowship. Back in the late 70s, Kreider figured he'd fill up the existing churches with the vanloads of young people he and others had won to Christ. Yet the young people never felt integrated in those existing churches. Kreider yielded to God's call on his life and in 1980 started DOVE (acronym for "Declaring Our Victory Emmanuel").

From a small, humble beginning the church grew to 2000 people in ten years. The congregation spread itself over a seven-county area of Pennsylvania.

Leading a megachurch would be a dream come true for most pastors. Kreider, however, realized that his megachurch was too

---

Instead of waiting for that perfect day to arrive, churches need to change their priorities now! Multiplication is high on God's desire list—the multiplication of leaders, groups, and churches.

---

complicated and cumbersome. It needed an injection of simplicity and reproducibility. It wasn't nimble enough to adjust quickly and raise up new generations of leaders. Kreider writes:

> If we wanted to build the church . . . we would have to give the church away. . . therefore, that is exactly what we did with our church. Giving our church away better suited our vision of a cell-based church planting movement intent on training a new generation of church planters and leaders. Our church in south central Pennsylvania became eight individual churches, each with its own eldership team. We formed an Apostolic Council to give

oversight to all the churches of DCFI. Then we gave each of the eight celebrations the freedom to become autonomous— they had the option of joining with the DCFI family of churches or connecting to another part of the body of Christ.[3]

The church has been giving itself away ever since. DOVE's commitment to simple, reproducible church planting is evident in its new openness to planting house church networks. Kreider's new book, *Starting a House Church*, reflects his innovative, forward-looking thinking. DOVE continues to plant cell-based churches and has now planted approximately 100 churches.

Growing to survive

Cactus is a staple of the desert. It flourishes in a dry, hot environment. Cactus, unlike other plant life, can absorb up to 800 gallons of water in just a few days. Only two hours after rain the formation of new roots help absorb large quantities of water.

Unless church plants organize around evangelism, no one will show up. After all, most Christians would rather worship in a full-service church where their needs are met.

Because of this innate ability, cactus can survive and flourish in the suffocating desert heat.

Church plants, like cactus, learn to survive in desolate environments. They learn to adjust their strategies to overcome harsh realities. Many larger churches don't have this same earnestness. Bob Roberts Jr., senior pastor of Northwood Church in Texas, has planted 100 some churches. In his book *The Multiplying Church*, he writes:

On more than one occasion, I've found myself in a group of mega-church pastors who make a statement like this: 'We need to partner to start some significant churches—we don't need to waste our time on these little churches of a hundred or two hundred.' They don't get it! I try to educate them, but, more often then not, to no avail. When they make a statement like that, they miss two things. First, they don't know their history. Where faith has exploded, it has never been because of the multiplication of mega-churches, but of smaller churches from 50 to 200. . . Second, they don't understand the nature of movements. Movements are personal and viral. Where movements have emerged, it hasn't been because of the large, but because of the small.[4]

Church plants need new people, new ideas, and new vision if they are going to emerge out of the darkness into the sunlight. Established churches tend to be more concerned about building upkeep, the personality of the new preacher, who's on the board, and the program schedule for the upcoming year. Established agendas and traditions shield long-established churches from realizing they too live in the desert. Often when desert realities sink in, it's too late.

Church plants are completely stripped of all illusions. Do or die. Reach out or close the doors. Invite or implode. Church planters are desperate for growth. Without growth, the church folds. This reality keeps church planters on their knees, crying out to God.

Unless church plants organize around evangelism, no one will show up. After all, most Christians would rather worship in a full-service church where their needs are met. Few modern-day Christians with families are willing to join a new church where programmed ministries don't exist.

In survival mode, church plants must exercise their muscles, and as a result, they become healthy and vibrant. Christian Schwarz in *Natural Church Development* reveals that church plants are more effective in every area (leading people to become Christ-followers, baptizing members, and ministering to needs). He writes:

If instead of a single church with 2,856 in worship we had 56 churches, each with 51 worshippers, these churches would, statistically win 1,792 new people within five years—16 times the number the megachurch would win. Thus we can conclude that the evangelistic effectiveness of minichurches is statistically 1,600 percent greater than that of megachurches![5]

Struggling to start a church does wonders for church planters. They are developed and honed in the crucible of church planting. Church planting has helped me to grow in my relationship with Jesus more than any other ministry I've been involved in.

I look back at my first church plant in 1983. I was a single pastor, fresh out of seminary and looking for my first senior pastorate. My ultimate goal was to be a career missionary with the Christian and Missionary Alliance. I had something to prove.

Struggling to start a church does wonders for church planters. They are developed and honed in the crucible of church planting.

The CMA asks potential career missionaries to test themselves at home before ministering overseas. As a general rule, they know from experience that those who aren't fruitful "here" won't make it "over there." Crossing an ocean doesn't change ministry effectiveness.

At that time I was tired from learning about ministry in school. I had also spent several years as an "intern" and "associate pastor." The CMA probably would have approved an associate position but deep down inside I would have been bored. I needed a new challenge. I had to get out of the classroom and the church building. What did I believe? What was my ministry philosophy? I could repeat the philosophies of other great ministers and get an A on the exam, but I had not created my own ministry from scratch.

I took the leap and decided to plant a church.

At that time the CMA was reclaiming the inner cities of America for Jesus. They even offered some money for church planting in the inner city. I volunteered to plant a church that I called Hope Alliance in the heart of downtown Long Beach.

The two words that best describe my five-year church planting experience in downtown Long Beach are "total engagement." Another phrase might be "stretched beyond measure." As a single pastor, I had to marry, bury, and everything else. Hope Alliance Church didn't exist. I had to discover those who would be part of it. The meeting place didn't exist. I had to find it. My ministry method was unknown. I had to determine it.

My relationship with God grew to new heights because I was so totally dependent on God's guidance for every step of the journey. My seminary knowledge faded quickly in the dark realities of inner-city life. I felt like the token white person among an ethnic sea. Most of my parishioners had drug backgrounds, which tempted them to fall away when government checks were issued at the end of the month.

I met my wife, Celyce, four years into the plant, and we were married on February 13, 1988. We returned from honeymooning in Hawaii and settled into our rented house, which was grand central station for the church plant. That same night we received a 3 a.m. phone call from one of the members, demanding urgent counseling. Welcome back.

As I struggled to plant Hope Alliance Church in downtown Long Beach, God molded and shaped me more than I had the church. He showed me that He truly was faithful. Out of the doubt and discouragement, He was able to grow something lovely. He also prepared me for the cultural rigors of missionary life in Ecuador.

Making room for leadership

Dave Coopersmith was "associated" with a huge church near Moreno Valley but was never involved. None of the pastors knew him. If he drifted spiritually, no one would recognize it. Dave longed for more. Our paths crossed, and we became friends. I asked Dave if he'd like to join me in planting Wellspring, and he jumped at the opportunity.

When we launched the church in my home in September 2003, Dave was there. And in eight months, Dave had launched his own life group. Leading a group motivated Dave to get to know his neighbors, pastor people, and prepare a lesson. He eventually multiplied the group and learned additional skills. Church planting thrust Dave into a leadership position—far different than attending a large, even exciting church. Dave has said repeatedly, "This church plant has forced me to get involved. I've grown spiritually as I've participated in ministry, and this is what I like best."

Leadership is always needed, desired, and welcomed in church plants. Jamey Miller, founder and senior pastor of Christ Fellowship, is a great example of how to raise up new leadership through church planting. CF started with the goal of church planting. Jamey Miller led the first group in his home in 1993. Jamey multiplied the group, which became a network of cells and eventually turned into CF, located in Fort Worth, Texas. CF has now multiplied into twelve church plants. There's always a need for new leadership—both at the cell level and for church planting. The mother church is large at 300 in worship attendance and twenty-five cell groups.

Miller's strategy is simple. Start small groups and then look for potential church planters from among those who can both lead a group and multiply it. Miller's church-planting emphasis flows from his understanding of Scripture that God's plan for glory on earth is connected to reproduction. "Living things multiply," Jamey told me. This kingdom principle is central to Miller's church planting strategy. He believes we should expect to see reproduction in all facets of church life—from disciples reproducing, to cell groups, to churches, and even movements of churches.

Christ's living presence is the key. Groups multiply through Christ's living presence, and then Christ continues to reach out through church planting. Miller said, "There's nothing like group life to raise up future leaders and cultivate a readiness for church planting." Future church planters need to start at the small group level to understand the church planting process—since the small group is a microcosm of the future church plant. Not all small group leaders will become church planters, but those who show potential in effectively leading a group, multiplying it, and then coaching the new multiplications have the basic ingredients for church planting effectiveness.

Jamey models what he believes. Fifteen years after launching the movement, he said to me, "I'm once again leading a group in my own neighborhood because I think it's essential to stay in the battle."

During the first five years at Christ Fellowship, all the church plants succeeded. Then, like all church planting movements, they started having false starts and failures—mainly because of leadership and character issues. The failures gave them insight into the nuances of leadership effectiveness—why some succeed and others fail. Jamey admitted, "I'm still trying to figure out what makes an effective church planter. I have come to realize that some people are only called to be leaders of tens while others will lead hundreds. Some probably aren't called to the demanding task of planting a new church."

I asked Jamey about the core requirements for future church planters. He said,

> Our basic expectations are that potential church planters are in a small group (leading and multiplying it) and are working out the core values of loving God and one another, as well as reaching those who don't know Christ. And yes, they must have a burning call to go and start a community of believers. Those basic things provide the grid for seeing how someone is progressing and helps the rest of the church give the "amen" when it's time to send the person on a church planting assignment.[6]

The harvest is what stirs Jamey to look beyond the comforts of his own church towards the fields. Jesus said, "The harvest is plentiful but the workers are few. Ask the Lord of the harvest, therefore, to send out workers into his harvest field" (Matthew 9: 37-38). Church planting at Christ Fellowship has provided the means for new leaders to reap the harvest.

Sharing brings life

Moreno Valley was once a dusty ghost town. It's now a thriving city because people came together to share water, energy, and services. Lone rangers rarely survive in the desert. Lone restaurants or hotels usually last a few months or might scrape by for a few years, but they soon become desert museums, curious spectacles of an entrepreneurial spirit that couldn't make it alone.

New churches add spiritual strength and vitality to existing ones. They stimulate a spiritual atmosphere that benefits everyone. Abe Huber, founder and lead pastor of the *Igreja de Paz* movement, plants churches on the doorstep of the mother church in northern Brazil. The strength of additional churches benefits everyone in the city.

I stayed at Abe's home in 2002 while doing a conference at his church. I found Abe to act more Brazilian in culture than American. After each evening service, for example, he preferred to hang out with fellow Brazilians into the wee hours of the morning. "That's just Abe," his coworkers told me.

Now Abe leads a church-planting movement that is winning and discipling thousands for Jesus in Manaus, a city of 1.6 million residents located on the north bank of the Rio Negro. Abe has integrated one-on-one discipleship into the church's training process. Each person who comes to a celebration service or a cell group is assigned a one-on-one mentor. The mentor and mentored meet weekly for encouragement and accountability. The mentor guides the new person to participate in additional training classes and to attend spiritual retreats that are part of the equipping process—called MDA (Micro Discipleship Strategy).

The goal is for each person in the church to plant an evangelistic cell group, to multiply it, and to eventually plant an Igreja da Paz church. This effort has resulted in planting hundreds of churches throughout Brazil. I was amazed to see many Igreja da Paz churches located just a few minutes from the 15,000-member mother church. Most of these local churches follow the MDA strategy, but it's not a requirement. Each church is self-governing, has their own place to meet, and maintains a fraternal relationship with the Igreja da Paz movement.

Huber is a gifted leader, able to guide the large mother church, but he realizes that many leaders don't have those same gifts. They will pastor much smaller churches. The key is reproduction—which starts one-on-one and continues out to the masses.

God might want your church to become a multiplication center—making disciples who eventually plant churches. You don't have to worry that planting a new church will damage the mother church. Huber's example shows that new churches do not hinder the mother church, but are a great help to its own growth and spirituality.

Satan promotes the fallacy that new churches will drive out the existing ones and hurt their attendance. Peter Wagner writes:

> A new church in the community tends to raise the religious interest of the people in general and if handled properly can be a benefit to existing churches. That which blesses the kingdom of God as a whole also blesses the churches that truly are a part of the Kingdom.[7]

Springs in the desert

Palm Springs is about a one hour drive away from where I live. Palm Springs, like Moreno Valley, is a desert community. The difference is that Palm Springs has natural tree-lined canyons. Why? Bubbling hot springs are part of its geography. God is able to create springs in the desert. He said in Isaiah 43:19-21:

> See, I am doing a new thing! Now it springs up; do you not perceive it? I am making a way in the desert and streams in the wasteland. The wild animals honor me, the jackals and the owls, because I provide water in the desert and streams in the wasteland, to give drink to my people, my chosen, the people I formed for myself that they may proclaim my praise.

The good news for the church planter is that the God who created the desert is also the God who created the oasis. He's able to make springs abound in dry, difficult places. He's the God of the impossible and delights in making something out of nothing. No matter how dry and desert-like the situation, He loves to provide living water that brings life instead of death.

Chapter Two

What is a Simple Church?

A few years ago, I preached in Zurich, Switzerland and praised Ulrich Zwingli in my sermon. Zwingli (1484-1531) was one of the great Swiss reformers who spread the doctrines of justification by faith and stood against the religious traditions of his time. Yet after the sermon, the pastor approached me saying, "In the next service, you probably shouldn't say too much about Zwingli. Just a few miles from our church is a river where Zwingli and followers drowned the Anabaptists."

Why were the Anabaptists persecuted? Because they wanted to take Zwingli's reformation to the next level. Anabaptists believed that justified, regenerated believers who were baptized as adults should meet together apart from the state church The Anabaptists longed for a reformed church—not just reformed doctrines.

When Martin Luther nailed his ninety-five theses to the door, he didn't plan to break from the Roman Catholic Church. His goal was to correct abuses in the church and make God's Word the foundation for faith and practice, not the pope's authority.

Luther's reformation didn't settle the question of the true nature of the church. Break-away groups, like the Anabaptists, wanted to practice Luther's doctrine in a church with like-minded people. They felt the state church was culturally bound and didn't conform to Scripture. Yet Luther vehemently opposed the radical reformers, and the debate about the nature of the church continued unabated.

Similar debates continue to this day.

Some denominations, for example, don't believe a church exists until an ordained pastor is in charge. Others won't officially recognize a church until there are enough charter members; still others believe a church must first launch a public gathering, say on Sunday morning, before the real church is present. Some go farther, demanding robes and rituals. Wolfgang Simson sums up this view: "The image of much contemporary Christianity could be summarized as holy people coming regularly to a holy place on a holy day at a holy hour to participate in a holy ritual by a holy man dressed in holy clothes for a holy fee."[1]

I am convinced that many of our church definitions are far too complicated.

What is the church?

The Westminster Confession describes the church with great eloquence:

Unto this catholic visible Church, Christ hath given the ministry, oracles, and ordinances of God, for the gathering and perfecting of the saints, in this life, to the end of the world: and doth, by His own presence and Spirit, according to His promise, make them effectual thereunto.[2]

Meanwhile the Southern Baptist's definition of the church is more down-to-earth:

A New Testament church of the Lord Jesus Christ is . . . an autonomous local congregation of baptized believers, associated by covenant in the faith and fellowship of the gospel; observing the two ordinances of Christ, governed by His laws, exercising gifts, rights, and privileges invested in them by His word, and seeking to extend the gospel to the ends of the earth.[3]

I mentored one doctoral student who wrote his dissertation about planting a simple church among the Christian Reformed denomination. He was looking for support and approval. He planned to begin with a one small group (cell) and multiply into more groups. His title, *A Strategy for Beginning a Church Multiplication Movement in Muskegon, Michigan*, declared his bold intentions.

But he first had to get his initial cell accepted as a real church. He searched the Christian Reformed documents to show that what he was planting—even from the first cell—was truly the church of Jesus Christ. He found a passage in the *Manual of Christian Reformed Church Government* that said, "Groups of believers, although too small to be organized, *do constitute the church* and are entitled to the love and care of the church through the ministrations of a neighboring council."[4]

His denomination defined **church** as a gathering of people in one place at a particular time, under a pre-determined pastoral role. His denomination—like most others—defined church according to the definition given by Luther, Calvin, Zwingli, and other reformers. Their view of the church was a *place* where the gospel was rightly preached, the sacraments rightly administered, and church discipline correctly exercised.

---

*I am convinced that many of our church definitions
are far too complicated.*

The challenge for the doctoral student was to find a way in which a small group or a house church could incorporate the marks of the church on the small group level (preaching the word, celebrating the sacraments, and practicing church discipline). He had to overcome the denominational rules that stated, "A minister of the word serving as pastor of a congregation shall preach the word, administer the sacraments, conduct public worship services, catechize the youth, and train members for Christian service." [5] Notice the words "conduct public worship services." Could he have a church without a public service? He planned to start the church with one small group. Was that not the church from the beginning? His struggle was not merely a theoretical exercise. He was looking for denominational funding and support.

He did an admirable job of describing point- by-point how the first small group would participate in the word of God, baptize new believers, partake in the Lord's supper, and even exercise Christian discipline. In effect, this doctoral student simplified the definition of the church.

Back to the basics

Charles Brock, well known church planter and trainer, once said:

> I believe a perverted and tarnished view of what a church is, constitutes one of the greatest hurdles faced by church planters. In the New Testament, the word 'church' was applied to a group of believers at any level, ranging from a very small group meeting in a private home all the way to the group of all true believers in the universal church.[6]

The Greek word *ekklesia* (assembly, gathering) infers that we cannot experience church until we come together. To make sure we benefit from the testimony of other believers, God has ordained the local church, which consists of believers connected in a particular city, town, or village. But what exactly is the local church? Alfred Kuen studied the topic in-depth and wrote *I Will Build My Church*:

> There does not seem to be a clear-cut way to define a local church. For example, is it when you have a constitution and regular meetings? Is it when you have baptized believers who partake regularly of the Lord's supper? Is it when you have church officers, such as elders and deacons? Should numerous norms be present in order to have a local church? It certainly does not include a certain level of maturity: for the Corinthians were yet carnal but Paul called them a church. . . When, then, can a body of believers be called a church? I personally tend toward a simple definition: a body of believers can be called a church whenever that groups meets together regularly for mutual edification."[7]

Christ's Church does not require layers of hierarchy, added later by religious institutions. But just what does it include? John

Dawson in his best-selling book, *Taking Our Cities for God,* writes:

> There is no absolute model for what a local church should
> be. I once spent an afternoon with over one hundred spiritual
> leaders from several denominations. We tried to come up with
> a universal definition of a biblical local church. You may think
> that it was an easy task, but if you consider all the culture and
> circumstances of people on the earth and you examine the
> diversity of models in the Bible, you will begin to understand
> our frustration. After many hours of discussion, we had
> produced many good models, but no absolute definition other
> than 'people move together under the lordship of Jesus.[8]

Paul called groups of believers *the church* before they had
appointed leadership. Paul and Barnabas had already established
churches in Lystra, Iconium, and Antioch on their first journey. So
on the second journey, Paul and Barnabas appointed elders. Acts
4:21-23 describes the situation:

> They preached the good news in that city and won a large
> number of disciples. Then they returned to Lystra, Iconium
> and Antioch, strengthening the disciples and encouraging
> them to remain true to the faith. "We must go through
> many hardships to enter the kingdom of God," they
> said. Paul and Barnabas appointed elders for them in each
> church and, with prayer and fasting, committed them to
> the Lord, in whom they had put their trust. After going
> through Pisidia, they came into Pamphylia, and when they
> had preached the word in Perga, they went down to Attalia.

Paul and Barnabas focused on those minimal qualities that made
up the church. They were intensely interested in gathering followers
of Jesus together under leadership. The churches that they planted
were simple and reproducible.

The assembly

Jesus says in Matthew 18:20, "For where two or three come together in my name, there am I with them." Looking at the broader context of Matthew 18 (specifically verses 15-35), we see that Jesus is teaching the disciples a lesson in how to deal with sin and forgiveness. He tells them that they should first talk to the person who has sinned, but if no reconciliation is found, then they should take one or two others and try again. "If he refuses to listen to them, tell it to the church; and if he refuses to listen even to the church, treat him as you would a pagan or a tax collector"(Matthew 18:17).

The word for *church* in Matthew 18 is the Greek word *ekklesia*. The context is clear that Jesus is referring to a larger assembly than the two or three that dealt with the first sin.

A church, therefore, should have more than two or three people, according to Matthew 18. But Jesus doesn't say how large the church should be. Ralph Neighbour, influential author and church planter, adds his own insight to Matthew 18:

> How large could that assembly be? I propose it consisted of a body of people small enough that all parties were in accountability to one another. I once had a woman in a traditional Baptist church I was pastoring who decided to move in with a man who offered to feed and keep her and her two teenage daughters in exchange for her sleeping with him. When I took it to the Deacons, they said, "Pastor, we don't know this woman except to greet her on Sunday morning. We have no power to deal with her." It was then I began to realize that Jesus could not have been referring to a blob of protoplasm called "church," but rather to the expression of *ecclesia* as body members. Was not Jesus defining the size of a body when He chose twelve to be His first community to dwell with while on earth? I feel we need to see the body of Christ in its most basic form as small enough for true community to be experienced."[9]

Jesus isn't talking about an impersonal, anonymous assembly in Matthew 18. He has accountability and church discipline in mind.

The assembly knew each other and could act responsibly to confront a brother or sister who had done something wrong.

In one church planting situation, I dealt with a member who was sexually abusing his child. Under the conviction of the Holy Spirit, he felt filthy for doing so, although he tried to keep his sin from his wife. This man was part of a small group and well known by those in the church. We told him to tell his wife, or we were going to do so. In this case we also had to get outside help because the child's welfare took precedence over everything else. We were able to deal with this man's sin because he was committed to believers who knew him and his situation.

I've also dealt with people who were not members of our church. One of my church members asked me to talk to Bobby, who attended a nearby megachurch. Bobby had committed adultery, encouraged abortion in the women he impregnated, and never admitted his sin. I told him to openly confess his sin to those involved and to talk with one of his church pastors. I later heard that he decided to remain anonymous in his church and not deal with the sin. As the years passed, Bobby has continued his sexual promiscuity but continues to attend his "church."

My understanding of church

My own convictions about the church have led me to a few basic principles that I believe the New Testament shows should be present in any given church.

First, the church should have more than three people as mentioned in Matthew 18:15-35.

Second, those in the church should be accountable to God-appointed leadership. This implies that the leaders will know the members and the members will have a relationship with the leaders. Hebrews 13:17 is clear, "Obey your leaders and submit to their authority. They keep watch over you as men who must give an account. Obey them so that their work will be a joy, not a burden, for that would be of no advantage to you."[10]

Being accountable to leadership requires commitment to the church (1 Corinthians 5; Galatians 6:1-2).[11]

Third, Scriptures make it clear that a church needs to operate under the lordship of Christ. As Lord, Jesus Christ is Savior of the church. The church serves Christ. Christ died and rose so that he would be Lord of both the living and the dead. An assembly of people is not a true church unless Jesus is Lord.[12]

Fourth, churches should participate in the sacraments of both baptism and the Lord's supper (see Matthew 28:18-20; 1 Corinthians 11).

These are all simple expressions of what the church is. The focus of the church is never the building but always the people. The true church consists of those who have placed their faith in Jesus Christ and live under His lordship.

When my home group comes together on Sunday evening, it's fully the church. We have God-appointed leadership, we meet regularly, we read God's word, we participate in the sacraments— at times in the home group and at other times when all the home groups meet together for a common celebration. We are under the lordship of Christ and accountable to one another. It's a very simple gathering—simple and reproducible. Our goal is to reproduce our simple church to the world around us—just like the early church.

When my father-in-law died in July 2008, we were having one of our home meetings. We were about to enter a time of praying for unbelievers (empty chair) when Celyce, my wife, received a phone call from her sister, Belinda, who relayed the news that their dad had died. We gathered around Celyce to pray for her as she wept. We comforted her in a sensitive, Spirit-led way, all the time rejoicing inwardly that Leo is now in heaven and free from pain. Celyce needed us, and the Spirit brought comfort through the members in a profound way. We experienced Christ's presence in a special way through the church.

Chapter Three

The First Simple Churches

I spoke at a seminar in Florida a few years ago. The host church asked me to speak to the staff, and one of the pastors inquired about his network of small groups. He wanted to know what he should do when his network reached the third generation of small group multiplication. He hoped to tap into my knowledge of small group coaching structures in mega churches. My mind raced through the different case studies and variables, but my answer was less than convincing—and I was supposed to be the expert on the topic! It suddenly dawned on me that the church needed to simplify. The members had become too bulky and complicated in their quest for mega church status. I boldly declared:

> Your church has become too complicated because you've grown too large. The fact that we're talking about multiple layers of generational multiplication says to me that you need to simplify the process. You need to plant new churches. Give away some of those layers of multiplication to a new church plant. Don't try to figure out how to keep them all under the same roof. God wants you to become a church planting movement—rather than growing your own church larger and larger.

I surprised myself by that answer. For many years I promoted complicated coaching structures in mega cell churches and wrote books that helped people figure them out. Yet I began to realize that very few churches were large enough to understand what I was writing about. It also dawned on me that smaller church plants had the added benefit of being far less complicated!

The New Testament church was simple and reproducible. The early house churches would gather together whenever possible. Often because of persecution, they operated underground. House churches multiplied into new houses, and eventually this simple system of multiplication effectively spread the gospel around the world.

Christ empowered the first Simple Churches

Christ presented the foundation of the church in Matthew 16:16-19 when he asked Peter how others were identifying Him:

> Simon Peter answered, "You are the Christ, the Son of the living God." Jesus replied, "Blessed are you, Simon son of Jonah, for this was not revealed to you by man, but by my Father in heaven. And I tell you that you are Peter, and on this rock I will build my church, and the gates of Hades will not overcome it. I will give you the keys of the kingdom of heaven; whatever you bind on earth will be bound in heaven, and whatever you loose on earth will be loosed in heaven."

Jesus built the church upon the *confession* of Peter—that He Himself is the Christ. The church is built on Jesus. And when Jesus left the earth, He promised to sustain His church through the Holy Spirit. Jesus said in John 14:15-18:

> And I will ask the Father, and he will give you another Counselor to be with you forever— the Spirit of truth. The world cannot accept him, because it neither sees him nor knows him. But you know him, for he lives with you and will be in you. I will not leave you as orphans; I will come to you.

The Holy Spirit is the One who empowers the Church to grow. Jesus called the Holy Spirit the "Spirit of Truth." The Spirit of Truth would guide the disciples to write down Christ's very words, which we now have in the New Testament. Jesus says:

But when he, the Spirit of truth, comes, he will guide you into all truth. He will not speak on his own; he will speak only what he hears, and he will tell you what is yet to come. He will bring glory to me by taking from what is mine and making it known to you. All that belongs to the Father is mine. That is why I said the Spirit will take from what is mine and make it known to you (John 16:13-15).

The Holy Spirit never changes, but some cultures are more receptive to God's message than others. Ecuador was a receptive culture, and it was relatively easy to win converts and make disciples. Those preaching and planting churches in Spain, however, experience a long, tough journey.

Tim and Marilyn Westergren began planting a church in Madrid, Spain in early 1994, and they can testify that it wasn't easy. [1]

The Spaniards in Madrid are generally a non-responsive and even resistant people group. Evangelical believers in Spain make up less than 1% of the population (estimates range between 0.2 and 0.6%). Considering that gypsies make up at least twenty-five percent of the evangelical population and that a considerable number are Hispanics from Latin America, the actual percentage of non-gypsy Spaniards who are born-again believers is extremely small. While it is possible to lead Spaniards to Christ, it usually takes time for this to happen. Most evangelical churches in Spain are small and have little impact on the society.

Tim discovered that the resistant culture caused stress fractures on the dynamics of the first pilot group. The lack of response and the many aborted conversions dampened the spirit of the group. He had to guard against small group diseases setting in when the group didn't multiply after two years. He had to continually preach the word and allow the Holy Spirit to soften unreceptive hearts.

Tim admitted that one of the greatest challenges is making long-lasting friendships with non-Christians. "I find that most people are friendly to a point, but it's hard to go to a deeper level with people. I think a lot of Spaniards are happy with the friendship and family contacts that they already have."

The hard soil of Spain made multiplication of groups through conversion growth very difficult. The opposition that new Christians encounter in Spain made it hard to disciple the new believers into the initial groups. Tim writes, "We have been pleasantly surprised by the number of conversions—but disheartened by the number who fall by the wayside."

In spite of the failures and setbacks, Tim had counted the cost and realized he was in it for the long haul because he understood that the soil was hard and that it took time for the seeds of God's word to bear fruit. Tim writes, "We are miles ahead in the lives of those who have traveled with us. I don´t think they´d ever go back to business as usual. This gives me satisfaction for the time when the Spirit of God moves in this land."

In 2003, the team transitioned the church plant, Comunidad de Fe, to Spanish leadership. The church is now a self-governing, self-propagating, and self-supporting congregation. Before Tim left, the church had grown to six groups—five adult groups plus a youth group. They also began a celebration service which had grown to about sixty people.

Tim began leading a church planting team in a city called Tres Cantos. At the time of this writing, they now have eight weekly groups and gather about sixty adults and children in their celebration service, which meets every other Sunday for teaching, worship, and the Lord´s supper.[2]

The New Testament church was simple and reproducible. The early house churches would gather together whenever possible. Often because of persecution, they operated underground.

The good news is that Jesus wants to see lives changed and church growth take place. And He is interceding in prayer to make it happen. The writer of Hebrews says in 7:25 "he [Jesus] always lives to intercede for them." Jesus said to His Father:

As you sent me into the world, I have sent them into the world. For them I sanctify myself, that they too may be truly sanctified. My prayer is not for them alone. I pray also for those who will believe in me through their message (John 17:18-21).

Indeed, the risen Jesus is praying for the church planter!

The church that Jesus established is simple and reproducible. It's founded on Jesus Himself and empowered by the Holy Spirit. Whether a church is planted in a receptive or resistant culture, the church planter can be assured that the Holy Spirit is working in the hearts and minds of people as the word of God is proclaimed.

Simple church planting in Acts

The early church's prescription for church planting was simple: meet in homes and gather together whenever possible for fellowship and to hear the apostle's teaching. Acts 2:42-46 tells us:

> They devoted themselves to the apostles' teaching and to the fellowship, to the breaking of bread and to prayer. Everyone was filled with awe, and many wonders and miraculous signs were done by the apostles. All the believers were together and had everything in common. Selling their possessions and goods, they gave to anyone as he had need. Every day they continued to meet together in the temple courts. They broke bread in their homes and ate together with glad and sincere hearts, praising God and enjoying the favor of all the people. And the Lord added to their number daily those who were being saved.

It was a simple experience. They found expression for their new found faith in the home environment. The presence of the Holy Spirit used the home atmosphere to testify to the new family, Christ's church. Meeting in homes brought faith down to daily living. The early church in Acts:

- met together daily
- were instructed in the apostles' doctrine

- experienced a deep fellowship together
- loved each other and shared their goods with each other
- broke bread with each other
- shared in prayer with each other

My favorite book on church planting is *Creating Communities of the Kingdom*. David Shenk and Ervin Stutzman, experienced church planters, write:

> We read that the church grew and multiplied exceedingly as neighbor told neighbor the news of Jesus Christ. We may assume that as the little living rooms became packed with people, the groups divided and new cells were formed. Soon the original 100 or so congregations multiplied and became hundreds of small group fellowships throughout the whole metropolitan area. They witnessed with power and persuasiveness to the saving acts of God.[3]

Imagine the electrifying atmosphere of the early church. Leaders and churches spontaneously multiplied and filled the city. Is anything like that happening today?

As I speak to people in ministry, I keep hearing about the effectiveness of the Antioch Community Church in Waco, Texas. Jimmy Seibert, the founding pastor of ACC, was radically transformed at the age of seventeen. He started small groups on the Baylor University Campus that eventually grew to 600 students on four campuses. He and some of the students wrote a book called *Reaching College Students through Cells*. In 1999 Jimmy started ACC.

ACC has sent thirty-eight church planting teams all over the world (to twenty-four nations) and have a missionary support staff from their own church of 450. ACC has never been content to grow one church larger and larger. Yet as the mother church gives itself away, it keeps growing (135 life groups and 2500 in worship attendance). Like the New Testament church, God has called them to become a church planting movement. Jimmy once told me that churches need to offer their people a practical missionary vision to reach the world. As a college pastor, he noticed that parachurch organizations were often more mission focused than the church. "God's plan is for the church to offer a world vision. Young people long to give themselves to a world-changing vision," Jimmy said.

ACC breathes the principle of multiplication—in their groups, leaders, churches, and missionaries. Each year ACC offers either a missions conference or a church planting conference on a rotating basis.

Antioch believes and teaches the need for brokenness and the filling of the Holy Spirit which result in radical obedience. *This church emphasizes very plain, clear biblical concepts.* I pressed Jimmy about what model he was following and he kept on coming back to their desire to follow biblical principles. "In my experience, the church at large doesn't do the simple, biblical things well, so we get caught up in following models," he told me.

Sean Richmond left ACC ten years ago to plant a church in Boston, Massachusetts. Like other church planters, Sean started a life group that multiplied and eventually turned into a once a month celebration service. As the life groups grew and multiplied, they eventually grew into a weekly celebration service. The church in Boston now has some twenty life groups and 300 people worshipping in a local high school gym. Yet their goal is to start a movement. They were excited to send out their first missionary church planting team to a restricted-access country.

Robert Herber, recently planted an ACC church in San Diego, California. Although brought up in a Christian home, he didn't start walking with God until becoming connected to passionate people from ACC at Baylor University. He also caught fire, grew in the Lord, and eventually raised support to plant a church (all church planters raise their own support). Like all church planters from ACC, Robert gathered together a team. The church planting team from Antioch joined together to start the first life group. Through the initial pilot group they prepared San Diegans to be the leaders of the future life groups. Their goal is to win as many people as possible to Jesus and to start life groups in the process. Robert writes, "Today two more students were saved: our next door neighbor and then the pitcher of the baseball team!"

The home life group is the basis for church planting at Antioch. It was also the foundation for early church planting. When we read the New Testament letters we often forget the context of those early believers. Paul was writing to house churches:

- Acts 12:12: "When this had dawned on him, he went to the house of Mary the mother of John, also called Mark, where many people had gathered and were praying."
- Romans 16: 3-5: "Greet Priscilla and Aquila, my fellow workers in Christ Jesus. They risked their lives for me. Not only I but all the churches of the Gentiles are grateful to them. Greet also the church that meets at their house."
- 1 Corinthians 16:19: "The churches in the province of Asia send you greetings. Aquila and Priscilla greet you warmly in the Lord, and so does the church that meets at their house."
- Colossians 4:15: "Give my greetings to the brothers at Laodicea, and to Nympha and the church in her house."
- Philemon 2: "Apphia our sister, to Archippus our fellow soldier and to the church that meets in your home."

When Paul wrote about believers serving each other during the Lord's supper, picture the context of the home. When Paul expounds on the operation of spiritual gifts, envision a house church environment. When he elucidates the role of each member in the body of Christ, imagine the warm atmosphere of the early house church. John Mallison writes, "It is almost certain that every mention of a local church or meeting, whether for worship or fellowship, is in actual fact a reference to a church meeting in a house."[4]

Most likely from ten to twenty people gathered in each of these home groups. Some scholars believe that there were probably 100-200 of these small congregations, meeting in homes throughout the Jerusalem area. They gathered together for celebration under the apostle's teaching (Acts 2:46). The New Testament and church history confirms that the church has historically followed both a small and large group structure (see appendix five for Bill Beckham's analysis of both the large and small group aspects).

When the early church could no longer openly meet because of persecution, the people primarily met in the homes.

Some have pointed out, however, that even after persecution the early house churches met occasionally for celebration gatherings. The love feast of 1 Corinthians 11 and Paul's visit to Troas in Acts 20:6-12 could be examples of joint celebration. House churches were the smaller circles of fellowship within the larger fellowship of the city church. Paul said, "To the church of God in Corinth, to those sanctified in Christ Jesus." He also writes in the same book to the individual house church: "Aquila and Priscilla greet you warmly in the Lord, and so does the church that meets at their house" (1 Cor. 16:19). Paul repeats this pattern in his epistle to the Thessalonians and to the Romans (1 Th. 1:1; 2 Th. 1:1; Rom. 16:23).

The warm, caring atmosphere of the house church prevailed for some four centuries. The world tried desperately to annihilate Christ's church through torture, terror, and endless persecution. In spite of fierce persecution, the early church continued to grow exponentially. The mighty Roman legions couldn't stop them and soon Christianity spread throughout the entire world. Jesus, the Lord of the Church, granted victory. Satan would have fared better against a large centralized church. But to destroy scattered house churches meeting throughout the empire, his task proved futile. The house church structure was simple enough to quickly scatter and regroup when persecution knocked at the door.

Paul and simple church planting

Paul was the most effective church planter of the first century. He planted simple, reproducible churches and moved on to spread the flame. At one point in his ministry, he said, "So from Jerusalem all the way around to Illyricum, I have fully proclaimed the gospel of Christ" (Romans 15:19). Before AD 47 there were no churches in these provinces. In AD 57 Paul spoke of his work being accomplished. Roland Allen, a British author who studied the life of Paul, writes:

This is truly an astonishing fact. That churches should be founded so rapidly, so securely, seems to us today, accustomed to the difficulties, the uncertainties, the failures, the disastrous relapses of our own missionary work, almost incredible.[5]

Paul believed in releasing leaders and moving on. He practiced simple church planting.

God's calling

Paul was called to preach the gospel and to plant churches. Acts 9:1-19 explains Paul's radical conversion and calling. Paul's calling wouldn't allow him to quit. He knew he would give an account to the Master, and he wanted to say what Jesus said to the Father, "I have brought you glory on earth by completing the work you gave me to do" (John 17:4).

Church planting is so demanding that those who engage it, like Paul, must be called by God. It's one thing to believe in a good idea, but good ideas come and go. When a person is called by God, he or she will stick with the idea until it's accomplished. A lack of a true calling by God is why many church planters give up.

In my first church plant, my seminary education had little bearing on my experiences. I remember pleading with Janie (not her real name) to use her welfare checks to buy food for her children rather than drugs for herself. I felt inadequate when I tried to plant a church among people like Janie. Since I lived about one hour from Fuller Seminary—at a time when church growth theory was in its heyday— I tried to learn about church planting from the many seminars and courses Fuller offered. I found myself bouncing around from one church growth technique to the next. My poor church bounced with me as I experimented with one failed innovation after another.

My problem was that none of the church growth literature really dealt with how to plant an inner city church. My area was one of the most ethnically diverse regions in California. Those who attended the church were white, black, Latino, and Asian. Some Sundays many showed up—other weekends the services looked like a ghost town.

Even though my context didn't apply to most of the church growth literature, which was coming out of the growing suburbs, I wanted success badly enough to try any method that promised results. One day I loved church growth, and the next I hated it.

Even though I was theoretically tossed like the waves of the sea, I could always fall back on the fact that God had called me to plant the church. The Bible was my guidebook. The Spirit kept me going.

Through it all, God stretched me and molded me. The feelings of failure only caused me to depend on Jesus Christ more. Where else would I go?

---

*Church planting is so demanding that those who engage it,
like Paul, must be called by God.*

Paul the apostle did not stray from his heavenly calling to plant churches. His vision to plant churches came about as a result of prayer, fasting, and reading the word. He constantly sought to know where that calling was leading him and in what direction it was taking him. In Acts 16:6-7 we read that Paul and his companions traveled throughout the region of Phrygia and Galatia, having been kept by the Holy Spirit from preaching the word in the province of Asia.

When they came to the border of Mysia, they tried to enter Bithynia, but the Spirit would not allow them to. Paul felt compelled to follow the Spirit's calling, even when difficulties and problems abounded.

In the midst of major obstacles, opportunities often present themselves. Paul said to the church in Corinth, "I will stay on at Ephesus until Pentecost, because a great door for effective work has opened to me, and there are many who oppose me" (1 Cor. 16:8–9). Those who opposed Paul didn't hinder him from walking through the open door. He knew God's calling on his life to plant churches. Nothing else mattered.

Paul's trials and troubles

Paul knew dangers and difficulties firsthand. He faced them continually. He was forced to defend himself against the attacks of false apostles by saying:

> Are they servants of Christ? (I am out of my mind to talk like this.) I am more. I have worked much harder, been in prison more frequently, been flogged more severely, and been exposed to death again and again. Five times I received from the Jews the forty lashes minus one. Three times I was beaten with rods, once I was stoned, three times I was shipwrecked, I spent a night and a day in the open sea, I have been constantly on the move. I have been in danger from rivers, in danger from bandits, in danger from my own countrymen, in danger from Gentiles; in danger in the city, in danger in the country, in danger at sea; and in danger from false brothers. I have labored and toiled and have often gone without sleep; I have known hunger and thirst and have often gone without food; I have been cold and naked. Besides everything else, I face daily the pressure of my concern for all the churches (2 Corinthians 11:23-28).

Church planting is difficult. It's easy to feel like a failure. Only church planters understand the inward emotional pain that comes from the lack of growth—the feeling that you haven't arrived. One church planter wrote me saying:

> I'm an Anglican (formerly an Episcopal) priest who planted a cell-based church in Tallahassee, Florida in 2002. The church has continued to grow in numbers, and we've seen lots of transformation. Still, it is slooooow. Currently we have 7 cells with about 50 people in them. When we began I thought it would take off and grow like wildfire. I fight continually with the inner demon that it and I are not "enough," that it is my fault that it hasn't grown quicker and the "if only" lie. Through the slow growth, however, I am learning to focus on being faithful and to give thanks for the changes I see in the lives of people.[6]

Bob Roberts Jr. writes, "Pastors who raise up other pastors and plant churches out of their church are generally pastors who have been broken. This brokenness generally results from a failed attempt to achieve their own dreams as opposed to God's."[7] Often people won't accept the church planter until they see his response in the battle—whether or not he takes God's plan seriously enough to rejoice in adversity.

I don't like to be weak. I want to be strong. Yet, in those times when people don't show up or when the projector fails, and I feel weak and helpless, God is the closest and the strongest.

I'll never forget the Christmas service of 2005. A young believer asked me the day before our service if he could give a brief testimony. *Why not, it will give us some variety,* I thought. He was a faithful brother, and I rejoiced that new people wanted to get involved.

At the end of the service, I gave him permission to share, and he started by handing out Christmas cards. *This is great,* I thought. Then he proceeded to say to our congregation, "I just wanted to announce that I'm leaving the church. You as a church have treated me very badly in a time when I needed help. You all know that I've been without a job, and you have not been there when I needed you. I'm leaving."

I tried to quell the damage by quickly standing up, putting my arm around the brother, and gracefully closing the service. But the damage was done, and the congregation was stunned. So was I. We were very small and couldn't afford a damaging testimony like that one. To make matters worse, another, more mature couple in the church had stirred up this brother against our church by gossiping to him. I immediately perceived that the larger problem was the gossiping couple who had far more influence on others in our congregation.

After the service and the days following, I persistently explained the reality of the situation to all parties. Several weeks earlier, the pastoral team had decided to give him $300, but one of the team members had forgotten to relay the information. My explanations didn't help too much—both the couple and the single man left the church.

Granted, we did learn huge lessons—one of them being the need to communicate more effectively. And as I look back, the departure of the gossiping couple was a blessing. I don't like influential people to leave, but influential gossipers—like this couple—can destroy a church.

Church planters reading this book know that the situation I just described is part of the church planting terrain. You just have to swallow and, with dependence on the leading of the Holy Spirit and God's word, get on with it. Keith Bates, a church planter in Australia writes:

> We started our church with the conviction that we would grow to be 1000 people in a town of 7,000. After almost ten years we are at thirty- something, but growing. I've been through about five years of deep discouragement, at times depression, in which I've thought about giving up. I've often felt like the Irishman swimming the English channel- he got 3/4 of the way across and turned back because it was too far to finish. I've realized that my faithfulness to God is far more important in his sight than my success; it's about obedience to His call not about whether I get bigger numbers than anyone else or not. [8]

All church planters experience feelings of failure that come from lack of growth—or wanting growth to come more quickly. Part of the loneliness comes from not knowing how or with whom to share those realties. Phil Crosson, a church planter in Oregon said:

> As a church planter, I know what it is like to be lonely. I didn't actually understand that or even appreciate that until I actually experienced it myself. The blank looks, the shrugs, it's all the same. I have come to learn a lot about me during those times. The main thing that I have learned is that I really don't want answers so much as I want understanding. What I mean is this. Often when I voice my loneliness, people will want to encourage me with good words or sound answers for me. All of that is fine, but usually when I am lonely, I just want understanding. [9]

While trials and troubles come when the church does not grow, they can also appear because of the growth. Ralph Moore, founder of the Hope Chapel movement, writes:

> A new church can be a magnet that attracts disgruntled Christians who have a history of conflict in other churches. My observations over the years tell me that more new churches fold from an inability to confront disruptive people than from any other cause. My own life was miserable until I learned to confront in love. I would avoid talking with difficult people. This failure on my part inadvertently gave them free reign over the church.[10]

Disgruntled people often make their way into church plants, trying to stake a claim to the initial work. Church planters have to be on guard for controlling attitudes in such people. Emotionally and spiritually unstable individuals are also attracted to new church plants.

Trials come in all shapes and sizes. Sometimes they come in the form of disgruntled people while at other times it's saying good-bye to those who were part of the church from the beginning but have chosen to go elsewhere.

Regardless of the type of trial, the church planter's family will also be impacted. For example, I travel all over the world and speak in vibrant churches. These engagements fill me up and compensate for any lack of excitement in church planting.

My wife and family, however, find their primary fellowship in the church plant. In the initial years at Wellspring, my wife struggled with not having an exuberant worship experience. She depended on Wellspring more than I did for her spiritual food. As a church plant, we couldn't offer her the dynamic experience she longed for. At times she had to depend solely on her time alone with God to nourish her.

And there's the question of children. Wellspring was the first plant I was involved in that included my own growing family. Whether my children liked it or not, they were part of the church planting trials. On various occasions, I can recall my kids' pain as they cried because they didn't have close friends in the church or because key people left the church (those they had grown to love and appreciate). The family of the church planter can't leave like others.

The church planter's attitude makes all the difference in the world. Although trials and difficulties abound, there are many wonderful opportunities to grow in the faith. Each of my daughters currently plays an instrument on the worship team, has been involved in worship dance, and has led a small group. God has used church planting to prepare them for future ministry.

Raising up new leaders

Paul developed Timothy as a leader by spending time with him in practical ministry (Acts 16:1-10). He then asked Timothy to take the next step by preparing others. Paul said, "And the things you have heard me say in the presence of many witnesses entrust to reliable men who will also be qualified to teach others" (2 Timothy 2:2).[11]

After raising up new leaders, Paul often revisited them to assure the quality control. He also prayed for them, wrote to them, and gave them counsel through his writings.

My good friend, Rob Campbell (Cypress Creek Church, Wimberley, Texas), has a network of seventy-three church plants around the world. Rob believes in raising up his people from within. One time I asked him if he'd be interested in a dynamic youth pastor who was floating his resume around. He said, "Joel, my conviction is to grow my leadership from within my church. I look for the faithful and fruitful ones who already know our church culture here at Cypress Creek."

Where does he find this leadership? College students. Cypress Creek Church has a fruitful ministry in neighboring city of San Marcos, home of Texas State University San Marcos. Cypress Creek prepares current students and recent graduates in small group ministry and then works with graduate students who desire to plant churches worldwide. They normally work with fifteen to sixteen college graduates at any given time. These students have demonstrated godly character qualities as well as the practical ability to reach unbelievers and multiply groups. The staff of Cypress

Creek take turns at meeting with these current students and recent graduates once per month for both coaching and training (e.g., they might read a book together, and so forth).

The ultimate challenge is to ask the potential church planter to rent an apartment and try to gather people together for a celebration service. The goal is to determine if the potential church planter can not only lead a small group and multiply it, but whether he or she is able to bring those small groups together in a celebration setting for the teaching of God's word.

Cypress Creek also finds churches or ministry organizations that have a similar DNA as Cypress Creek. They help those churches grow and prosper. Then they ask if the church would be willing to send someone to help Cypress Creek start a church in another place.

The church planters who Rob raises up continue their accountability relationship with Rob, his fellow pastors, and his network of churches.

The church planter's attitude makes all the difference in the world. Although trials and difficulties abound, there are many wonderful opportunities to grow in the faith.

Although Paul cared for the leaders of the churches he and his co-workers planted, he depended on the Holy Spirit to guide the churches he planted.

The fact is that Paul planted churches and then moved on—even allowing young converts to care for the churches. Paul preached in a place for five or six months and then left a church behind. He preached in Lystra for about six months on his first missionary journey, and then he appointed elders and left for about eighteen months. He came back and visited the church in Lystra for two months and left again. After three years, he visited them again but only stayed for one month.

Paul probably stayed in Thessalonica for six months, and he did not visit the church again for over five years. Yet he writes to "the church of the Thessalonians" and speaks of this church as being on the same footing as "the churches of God in Judea" (see 1 Thessalonians 1:1; 2:14).

At Corinth, he spent a year and a half during his first visit and then did not go there again for three or four years. Yet he wrote letters to a fully equipped and well-established church. Roland Allen writes:

> Paradoxical as it may seem, I think that it is quite possible that the shortness of his stay may have conducted in no small measure to St. Paul's success. There is something in the presence of a great teacher that sometimes tends to prevent smaller men from realizing themselves. By leaving them quickly, St. Paul gave the local leaders opportunity to take their proper place, and forced the church to realize that it could not depend upon him, but must depend upon its own resources.[12]

One of the ways that Paul taught people was through mutual encouragement. Everyone had the opportunity to minister. The power of the Holy Spirit and Christ's living presence was sufficient to sustain the young churches.

In the book *Heavenly Man,* Brother Yun talks about church planting in modern day China. God called him to start an "oil station"—a training center to send out church planters throughout China. These simple workers gathered in a cave to pray, study God's word, and learn to love one another. They had little food and less money. Yet, the Holy Spirit prepared them to become simple church planters who eventually spread over the Henan province of China. Through the planting of simple house churches, 123,000 people were baptized in just two years. Through God's protection and guidance and the Spirit's conviction, many became Christ-followers, and so many churches were planted they could not be counted.[13]

Section Two

Simple Church Principles

Chapter Four

Do You Have What It Takes?

John Varrelman felt God calling him at the age of nineteen to the pastorate. He volunteered for practically everything at his home church, New Life, in Puyallup, Washington. He also worked hard to earn a bachelor's degree in theology from Southwestern University.

After graduation, John unsuccessfully tried to find a pastoral position near his home church. He was thankful for the opportunities to preach at New Life but longed for something fulltime. God blessed him with his FedEx day job to pay the bills and support his wife Janet. Someday he would also need to support a family, so working a marketplace job was important.

John's frustration of not being in fulltime ministry, however, increased daily. "I really want to be a pastor," he confessed to Janet. "I just don't see myself working at FedEx much longer."

Then it happened. John attended a church planting conference in Tacoma, Washington. He sensed a burden for those without Christ and realized how important it was to start new churches. Church planting would give him the perfect opportunity to spread his wings—and maybe even start his own movement of churches. He didn't consider himself to be entrepreneurial—or even a strong people person. Yet at the conference he was challenged to believe God could use anyone.

Janet was willing but hesitant. She peppered John with practical questions, but John's vision and excitement stirred her to say yes. They were both ready to *go for it*.

In the weeks and months following, John bought everything he could find about church planting, including books recommended at the conference. He was thrilled that pastor Mark at New Life Church was willing to provide $200 per month for the first two years. "Sorry that we're not able to give you any people at this time. You know that our attendance has been way down this year."

John knew southern Seattle, having lived there for five years before moving to Puyallup. He figured it would be the perfect place to plant the church. He and Janet moved there in July and began making friends with their neighbors. Two months later they opened a Bible study in their home. Three people showed up. After distributing fliers in the neighborhood, two more began attending.

John's real focus, however, was the February launch date. Both he and Janet felt that Sunday services would give needed visibility and bring more visitors. They found a local community center to rent and spread the message about the first Sunday service.

Fifty-five people attended the first Sunday in February. John was thrilled! Although twenty were visiting from New Life, John was confident that all the dynamics were in place for continual church growth. John loved preaching. *I've found my calling in life,* he told himself. In the next four months, attendance wavered between twenty-five and thirty-five, even though John spent hours posting fliers, sending out advertisements, and working the Internet.

John never considered himself a "numbers" person and vigorously opposed the church growth success syndrome. Yet, as the months wore on, he admitted feelings of failure. *Where were all the people who committed themselves to show up each week?* He grew to dislike Sunday morning services because he found himself consumed with those who weren't there. He felt as if he was pushing a heavy cart up a steep hill. The excitement from planting a church was gone; now his focus was survival. He dreaded telling his friends and fellow pastors about what was happening at the church. He felt like a failure.

Eight months after starting the church, a key family left to attend a nearby megachurch, reducing the attendance from twenty-five to seventeen. Then another family left. When seven people showed up one Sunday, including Janet, he was beside himself. After enduring the same low attendance for several months, and an increasingly negative attitude among members, John and Janet decided to close the church. Church members encouraged him to move on. He tried to put a good face on the decision by telling friends and family that it was the "will of the Lord." Yet, inwardly, he cried out to God and felt embarrassed.

John and Janet's experience is quite common. And the pain is intense. Is there a way to know in advance who will successfully plant churches?

Is there a specific church planting gift?

If John Varrelman had demonstrated the gift of teaching, would more people have flocked to hear him? After all, Chuck Swindoll's church grew rapidly as droves of people came to hear Swindoll preach. I heard Chuck Swindoll preach once when he was pastoring in Fullerton, California and went away amazed at his powerful teaching. He reeled off crystal clear, riveting illustrations that allowed me to peer through the windows of difficult Bibles passages. No wonder people crammed in the church to hear him! But John Varrellman was no Chuck Swindoll.

And what about the gift of apostleship? Most of us would agree that Paul the apostle was thoroughly gifted to plant churches. Many look at Paul as the greatest church planter of all time. The word *apostle* was used in ancient times to refer to an admiral over a fleet of ships, which, under orders from a ruler, would start a colony. Apostles in that day had great authority to start colonies in foreign lands. In the New Testament, the apostolic gift applied to church planters like the apostle Paul, who pioneered new territories for the Gospel (Romans 16:7; 1 Corinthians 12:28–29). Church planters would certainly benefit from having the gift of apostleship and those who demonstrate this gift have an advantage when it comes to planting churches.

The gift of evangelism would also be a great help. And what about the gift of leadership? Perhaps John Varrelman lacked the confidence of a leader that would have kept people coming back each week.

It also seems that the gift of pastoring or teaching would energize a church planter to minister effectively to those in the congregation—

and attract more each Sunday. And who could argue that the gift of service or mercy wouldn't be beneficial?

I don't believe that one particular gift determines whether a person is qualified to plant a church. All twenty-one gifts that Paul lists in the New Testament could benefit a church planter in some way (1 Corinthians 12-14, Ephesians 4, Romans 12).

In addition, God often blesses people with more than one gift. He also can sovereignly distribute a new gift to a person in time of need.[1]

I don't believe that one particular gift determines whether a person is qualified to plant a church

---

Do you need a particular personality type?

John Varrelman's personality was more timid than outgoing. People called him a good friend. He established long-term relationships but didn't excite a crowd when entering a room.

Some have pinpointed church planting effectiveness and personality types. Aubrey Malphurs, a church planting expert and author of *Planting Growing Churches*, believes that the leader of the church planting team needs either a high D (driver) or high I (inspiration) personality style. Other team members could have a wide variety of styles, such as S (steady) or C (conscientious).[2] Malphurs bases his conviction on various church planting studies, one of them being a study of the DiSC personality test administered to a group of church planters.*

In this particular study, the personality types of sixty-six church planters were correlated with the growth of their churches. The

---

* DiSC personality types:

D: driver (decisive, independent, efficient, practical, determined)

I: inspiration (stimulating, enthusiastic, dramatic, outgoing, personable)

S: steady (supportive, willing, dependable, reliable, agreeable)

C: conscientious (thorough, persistent, orderly, serious, industrious)

survey revealed that the high D (driver) planters had an average attendance of seventy-two after the first year and 181 after an average of 5.2 years. Those with a high "I" (inspiration) had an average of ninety-eight after the first year and an average of 174 after 3.6 years. The high S (steady) had an average of thirty-eight after the first year and seventy-seven after 6.3 years, while the high C (conscientious) had an average of thirty-nine after one year and seventy-one after 4.3 years."[3]

It does seem logical that an extrovert with a more commanding personality would do better at attracting and sustaining a crowd. Yet, my good friend, David Jaramillo, certainly doesn't have an inspiring, driving personality, but he is a smart, steady administrator. He successfully discipled and raised up fifty small group leaders and the church grew to 600 in attendance, as well as planting four churches.

Then there's Mario Vega, senior pastor of the second largest church in the world. Mario is an introvert. I've spent a lot of time with Mario on many different occasions as we co-taught seminars. Mario rarely talks. Yet, under Mario's leadership the Elim Church in San Salvador, El Salvador has grown to approximately 11,000 home groups and 100,000 people attending those groups!

And what about those planting house churches? People who effectively lead house churches don't need to attract large crowds. Jim Egli, a small group researcher, administered the DiSC personality test among 200 small group leaders at Bethany World Prayer Center. After examining the research, he concluded:

> This initial research seems to show no strong correlation between DiSC personality types and cell growth. Ninety-eight percent of Bethany's leaders had taken the DiSC test and knew what their primary and secondary traits were, but no particular type performed better.[4]

Egli found that both extroverted and introverted personality types were equally effective in growing and multiplying small groups.

Granted, it's one thing to lead a small group, yet it's quite another to pull those groups together into a celebration service and sustain that growth. Jeannette Buller, an experienced church planter and coach, writes, "Starting something from scratch is a horse of a different color. Church planting involves making something happen that isn't currently happening. It requires a certain creative energy that not everyone has."[5]

Effective church planters have an uncanny mix of personality, gifting, and natural talents that help the person persistently lead the church to fruitfulness. While finding the right person might be subjective, there are certain characteristics that church planters possess. Charles Ridley is one person who has researched successful church planting more than anyone else.

What characteristics are important in church planters?

Dr. Charles Ridley, a leading pioneer in church planting assessment, conducted a study of church planters in the United States and Canada to determine the characteristics of successful church planters. The one phrase that characterizes his research is: *The best predictor of future behavior is past performance.* From his research and field testing, he developed a list of thirteen characteristics of effective church planters:

1. Visionizing capacity: Ability to project a future vision and bring the vision into reality.
2. Intrinsically motivated: Approaches ministry as a self-starter and works hard.
3. Creates ownership in ministry: Instills in the people a sense of personal responsibility for the growth and success of ministry.
4. Spousal cooperation: Effectively integrates ministry with family life.
5. Reaches the unchurched: Develops rapport with unchurched people and eventually connects them to church life.
6. Effectively builds relationships: Takes the initiative in getting to know people and deepening relationships.
7. Committed to church growth: Values church growth as a method for building more and better disciples; strives to achieve

numerical growth within the context of spiritual and relational growth.

8. Responsive to the community: Adapts the ministry to the culture and needs of the local residents.

9. Utilizes the giftedness of others: Equips and releases people to do ministry according to their spiritual gifts.

10. Flexible and adaptable: Ability to adjust to change and ambiguity.

11. Builds cohesiveness in the church body: Enables the group to work toward a common goal and skillfully handles divisiveness and disunity.

12. Demonstrates resilience: Ability to sustain oneself emotionally and physically through setbacks, losses, disappointments, and failures.

13. Exercises faith: Translates convictions into personal and ministry decisions.

A behavioral assessment was developed to discover which church planters possess these characteristics in abundance. The assessment doesn't ask questions like "What do you think or believe?" Rather the questions are more like, "Tell me a time when you developed a relationship with an unsaved/unchurched person." Again, the premise is that the best predictor of future behavior is past behavior. Anybody can say, "Oh yes, I believe the church should be reaching the unchurched," but if the person's past behavior doesn't match the theoretical statement, chances are the person won't behave differently in the future.

Ridley's assessment is not a fill-in-the-blank type test. Success depends on the trained assessor's ability to recognize the church planting characteristics in the potential church planter. No assessment is fool-proof. Some church planters have failed the Ridley assessment and have gone on to plant dynamic churches. Others scored very high and failed.

Those who assess others offer recommendations to the potential church planter—not scientific surety of their success or failure. As a safeguard, the assessment interview is often done with a team of two to five people so that it's not just one person's perception. The recommendation comes out of the group discernment.[6]

No one will score perfect "tens" in each category. There is no such thing as the perfect church planter. Ed Stetzer writes:

> Most church planting leaders would acknowledge that a new church is more likely to fail when it is started by a planter who has not been assessed. All other factors being equal, an assessment assures the selection of better church planters with a higher likelihood of success.[7]

John Varrelman was not interviewed before planting the church. But looking back, he now realizes that such an assessment would have alerted him to certain danger signs. For example, John couldn't remember a time in his past when he initiated a gathering on his own. He was more of a follower than a leader, enjoying one-on-one relationships with people.

Is it necessary to take a church planting assessment?

I didn't always believe in church planting assessments. I even resisted them. They seemed mechanical and unnecessary.

Then I planted the church in Moreno Valley. I knew from the beginning that my role was limited. I could only be the volunteer pastor because I was traveling ten weeks out of the year and my primary calling had shifted.

To compensate, we hired a fulltime associate pastor who we hoped would become lead pastor of Wellspring. This person felt "called" to join us and everything seemed to fall into place.

It soon became apparent, however, that he was not a gatherer. He was an excellent pastor and worship leader, but he didn't have the catalytic mix to gather people together—and that's what we needed in those initial stages of our church plant. At my prompting he made more than 750 contacts in the community during the first several months but was unable to draw them into the church.

Even after noticing he wasn't the catalytic type, we decided to give him two more years to see if he could earn his salary from the fruit of his ministry. We took our cue from denominations that often give their church planters a two-year salary and then expect the planter to live off the offerings of the church. At the end of the two years, he left Wellspring to find a role as pastor of discipleship and worship—a role that fit his calling and gifting.

As I look back, an assessment would have given me a better understanding of his gifts and abilities, and a realistic view of what I could expect from his ministry.

We did learn important lessons during that time period—specifically the type of person we needed at our church. God was good to help us find a catalytic gatherer in Eric Glover. I gladly turned the lead pastor role over to him, while taking on the role of coach and church planting pastor.

All other factors being equal, an assessment assures the selection of better church planters with a higher likelihood of success.

Bob Logan and Jeannette Buller have put together an excellent tape series and training manual called *Cell Church Planter's Guide* (ChurchSmart). Bob Logan, a church planting expert, points out that the lead pastor of a cell-celebration church planting team should have catalytic leadership skills. Other members of the team might have a wide-array of gifts and talents, but the lead pastor is different. According to Logan and Buller, some leaders are able to start one or two groups but are not gifted at pastoring the growth of the church beyond those first groups.

Many simple churches won't see the need for the same leadership characteristics that we at Wellspring were looking for. I talked to the leader of a house church planting movement who at one time offered the Ridley test but stopped doing so. He told me:

There are two reasons that we are not assessing our planters using this system. 1.) We are not paying them and so there is less investment of money and less need for insurance that the planter will be successful in a self sustained church in a given amount of time. 2.) Most of our planters are home grown, so we know them. They are already proven leaders. It is not always true that they are home grown, and when they are not, there is still limited risk in beginning an organic church. As they begin one or more churches, time will tell if they are to become leaders of a movement.

Tim Rowntree, co-founder of www.multiplyingchurches.org, administered Ridley's survey for many years but discovered some problems. He observed that Ridley's analysis was not able to analyze church planters who might want to plant networks of simple churches. Rowntree developed an adapted analysis for church planters called the *360 Assessment*. This new assessment evaluates different levels of church planters—all the way from planting simple house churches to gathering a larger group of people together in a church plant.

In chapters seven through ten I talk about different degrees of simplicity in church planting and how to begin well. John Varrelman launched his church before establishing a true core and, therefore, was weighted down by Sunday gathering of people who didn't want to be there. I'll share in later chapters that there is another way to plant an effective church.

Most would also agree that the call of God is more important than any type of assessment. The apostle Paul never took Ridley's test. And ultimately the potential church planter needs to be honest with himself or herself. Malphurs wisely counsels:

We are the ones, ultimately, who determine the accuracy of any assessment program. We can use such highly valid and sophisticated tools as the Personal Profile or the Myers-Briggs Type Indicator, but they only reflect the information that we supply. If that information is based on who we want to be or who someone else thinks we are, and not on who we really are, then it tells us nothing. Another factor that affects the accuracy of assessment is ministry experience. The more ministry experience people have, the more accurate will be their assessment of themselves. We know our leadership abilities best when we take advantage of opportunities to lead.[8]

All things considered, I do believe that assessing a church planter benefits both the church and the church planter.

Of the thirteen Ridley characteristics, perhaps the most critical to church planting effectiveness is the relationship between the church planter and his spouse or family.

The husband and wife team

John and Janet Varrelman had a great marriage. They took regular date nights and committed themselves to prioritize marriage over ministry. Many don't.

I think of one church planter who sent out the following emails as he was preparing to launch a church in Nevada. The flow of emails within a two month time period went like this:

- "We have been putting out door hangers in nearby neighborhoods and have sent out a 50,000-piece mail out to let folks know about services. Pray that these invitations would get into the right hands and would draw in a mighty harvest."
- "All systems in place: Please pray for the installation of the sound and lighting systems for the church. There is also a team building the stage for the auditorium that we will use. Pray that they will get this completed in time."
- "Praise God we had twelve families visit from the mailout and doorhangers we sent out."
- "Pray for clarity on how to get the word out in the area about the church."

Then I received the following email:

- I heard God saying that the church was not "viable" and that He had somewhere else for me to serve. Obviously this was shocking and difficult to hear, but I felt I should evaluate this with the organization that has primarily been funding this new work.

When I inquired why he quit so early in the process, he told me that his spouse wasn't in agreement. When the pressure mounted because of all the required work, this particular church planter found his marriage faltering. It was either the church plant or his wife. He chose correctly and decided to save his marriage.

Church planting will involve everyone in the family. Both the husband and the wife must be called. Jesus told us to count the cost before making a decision to follow Him. Counting the "church planting cost" means that both husband and wife are in one hundred percent agreement before starting the church. Church planting probably will be more demanding and rigorous than ever imagined. Be prepared.

John Varrelman now looks back at his church planting experience with amusement—and even joy. The trials and struggles he experienced have prepared him for his current market-place ministry. He's self-employed, leads a home group, and plays a key role in a growing church in Seattle that has now planted three daughter churches. John teaches one of the sessions for future church planters and often mentions his own failures. He knows from experience the dangers of lone-ranger church planting and is quick to promote team ministry. He also believes strongly in gathering a larger, stronger core in home groups before beginning a weekly celebration. What he and Janet learned through the hard-knocks of experience, they freely pass on to others.

Root System 101

I killed a tree. I'm embarrassed to say it, but a tree at the side of my house is dead, and I caused its untimely death. The tree is a monument of my over zealousness to rid the yard of stray roots and pesky weeds. I killed it by applying too much weed killer to remove the weeds at the tree's base. I probably inflicted the most damage, however, by cutting the tree's roots that had popped up above the ground to ruin my grass. Through it all, I learned an important lesson about tree roots. Don't mess with them. They're too important for the absorption of water and the transfer of inorganic nutrients. They also anchor the tree to the ground and can sometimes grow as deep as the tree is high.

Just as a tree depends on an extensive root system, great church plants depend on unseen principles and values that anchor them to a firm foundation.

Prioritize prayer

The first and most important root to cultivate is prayer. Paul the apostle said at the end of his life from a prison in Rome:

Devote yourselves to prayer, being watchful and thankful. And pray for us, too, that God may open a door for our message, so that we may proclaim the mystery of Christ, for which I am in chains. Pray that I may proclaim it clearly, as I should. Be wise in the way you act toward outsiders; make the most of every opportunity. Let your conversation be always full of grace, seasoned with salt, so that you may know how to answer everyone (Colossians 4:2-4).

Most church planters are pragmatic. They want to know what will work. *Immediately.* Most are fascinated by techniques that promise quick growth.

Yet, the only church worth planting is the one that God himself brings to life. And such a plant requires prayer at its very foundation— the root level. Only God can break down the cultural resistance to New Testament Christianity. A church cannot survive without prayer. Norman Dowe, an experienced church planter, writes:

> I have failed at planting a church twice. My first reaction is to blame my lack of giftedness on my failure. I am a pastor/teacher not an evangelist, nor an apostle. After my last fiasco, the Lord took me to Zech. 4:6 in the context of Jerubbabel rebuilding the temple. I failed not because of my gift but because of my reliance on my experience, training, and reading. I failed because I did not rely on the Spirit. I am no longer infatuated with structures but am trying to replace that with true spirituality. I read once that Cho was asked the secret to his success. He said, "I pray and obey."[1]

God is raising up a multitude of church planters who "pray and obey." They are declaring, "We won't even go on unless you are leading, oh God."

When Rob Campbell planted Cypress Creek Church in Wimberley, Texas, he made prayer his first priority. He not only exemplified prayer but hired Cecilia Belvin, the pastor of prayer, as the first staff person. Today Cypress Creek Church has one of the most vital prayer ministries in existence. God has blessed this church abundantly because they've placed Him first.

Most books on church growth focus on techniques and insights to attract and keep non-Christians. Many of these books say very little about prayer. Peter Wagner, church growth guru, admits that for too long church growth theory has been dominated by techniques. "Not too long ago, I am embarrassed to say, it would have been quite difficult to find a church growth book that placed the spiritual aspect of planning front and center in more than a token way."[2]

Above everything else, church planting is a spiritual battle. Satan and his demonic hordes laugh at powerless, prayerless churches. These same dark forces become extremely worried when churches commit to fervent and effectual prayer.

God is raising up a multitude of church planters who "pray and obey." They are declaring, "We won't even go on unless you are leading, oh God."

I recommend that a church planter first call together a group of intercessors to pray for God's guidance and blessing every step of the way. Then gather others in the church to pray for every detail of the church's life. Continue praying throughout the entire church planting project. Scripture says, "Unless the Lord builds the house, its builders labor in vain" (Psalm 127:1).

At Wellspring, we've tried to practice prayer from the beginning. We pray every Thursday at 7 p.m, and then once a month we have a half-night prayer meeting. We decided to make prayer a core value of our church from the very beginning.

Prayer is the key to church planting. It is the basis for everything that takes place.

The church plant starts and continues with prayer.

Concentrate on core values

There are different types of roots. Aerial roots, like ivy, rise above the ground. Structural roots are the large roots that support woody plants and trees. Surface roots go below the soil, finding water and easily available nutrients. Tuberous roots, like sweet potatoes, allow a portion to swell for food or water storage.

Trees and plants don't decide what root structure will suit them best. Those decisions are part of their DNA. In the same way, churches have their own coding or DNA. While God's word is the same for all Christ-centered churches, each church needs to determine its core set of values.

Here I'm referring to a church's philosophy of ministry and priorities. And each church will have specific traits that reflect their unique environment. When developing Wellspring, we discerned specific points that fit our convictions and culture. We began to pray and talk about those unique characteristics. Several themes developed:

- **Prayer emphasis.** God wanted us to do everything through prayer. This was a key Wellspring value that we've promoted since the church's beginning.
- **Gather the core first.** God showed us that we should first grow the groups and leaders who would eventually become the crowd. We believe that as leaders are trained and released, the church will grow naturally. As the small groups grow and multiply, we will come together more often for joint celebration worship.
- **Ethnic emphasis.** The ethnicity of Moreno Valley is approximately 40% Hispanic and 30% Caucasian, while the rest is divided between Asian and African-American. We wanted to see this reality reflected in the church plant.
- **Equipping Track priority.** We believe that everyone in the church should be trained. We prepared a specific training course of five books.[3] Everyone in the church is expected to participate in the training.
- **Coaching.** Coaching small group leaders is a key component of what we do. Each leader needs a coach. It's essential not to leave small group leaders dangling on their own. Each one needs care and ministry. We coach leaders both individually and as a group.
- **Church Growth.** We believe that God wants to win lost men and women to Jesus Christ and to disciple them through His church. We believe it's wrong to seek personal success in ministry. While personal success and ambition have nothing to do with God's desire to grow His church, we've come to realize that an ambition for church growth is God's ambition to reach a lost world. God

wants the church to grow in order to reach men and women for Jesus Christ and see them turned into disciples. It stems directly from God's heart. Our will has to be aligned with His will.

Other pastors I've worked with have chosen: relational evangelism, leadership development, community/fellowship, and multiplication as their core values. I think it's important to discern what you're already passionate about—the roots that God has already given to you. Each church planter needs to pray and decide what God is calling the church to emphasize.

Establish leadership

Tree roots grow before the tree top appears. They cover a large, unseen area—often two to three times larger than the visible area. Like roots, effective church plants first develop the leadership structure before the rest of the church appears.

A common problem in church planting is when a man or woman of God struggles all alone to build the church. David Shenk writes:

> The Acts record suggests that the ministry was always carried forward by a team. They apparently never commissioned a missionary to go alone into a new region to plant churches. A noteworthy example is the commissioning of Paul and Barnabas, accompanied by John Mark, as missionaries to the Gentiles. These men were commissioned by the church in Antioch to plant churches among people who had never heard the gospel.[4]

Not only was Paul part of a team of workers who planted churches, but he also appointed teams of leaders to guide those churches in his absence. Although Paul called these leaders by the different names of elder, overseer, and pastor, most likely he was referring to the same person (each of the titles emphasized a different aspect of the leader's function).[5]

Paul was not content with appointing one leader for each church. In every place he appointed several. This ensured that all the authority wouldn't be held by one person. Malphurs writes:

The days of the specialist who attempts to minister without a team in the context of the typical church are numbered. If these church plants survive, most will remain small and drain the leader's energy and the sponsor's finances.[6]

I recommend that church planters choose their leaders (e.g., elders) from among the small group leaders. Since these leaders are already in ministry and are pastoring the church with you, they are the logical choice to serve on the leadership team. At Wellspring, only life group leaders serve on the leadership team. Our life group leaders have passed through the equipping process and have proven themselves in battle. I don't believe all small group leaders should be part of the leadership team, but we do pick them from that pool. The church planter is then the principal leader of the leadership team.[7]

Along with the leadership team, I consider it wise to have an accountability team, which I refer to as the "administrative team." I don't believe a church planter should be handling the church finances because this is the job of the administrative team. Church planters need protection from the perception of mishandling "administrative functions."

The team should model Christ's call for unity among His followers to the rest of the church. Even Jesus modeled team ministry when he guided the twelve for three years. If the team does not get along, why would others in the congregation commit to the unity of the body that Christ calls us to? When a leadership team is divided in spirit or purpose, the congregation will reflect that division.

Raise funds

Roots are often restricted by rocks or compacted soil below the surface—or as in the case of the dead tree outside my house, by people. Funding can be a complicated problem because it goes deep down to the depth of our subsistence and survival. Church planters need to find creative ways to support themselves. Paul argued that missionary church planters should be paid for their service

(1 Corinthians 9:14), and he also embraced long-distance support (Philippians 4:10,14-18). He also worked as a tentmaker (Acts 18:3). The varied ways that Paul received support opens up a wide range of possibilities for church planters. One possibility is for a church planter to raise support.

Raising outside support

Many church planters ask people to support them for a specific period of time. All church planters at Antioch Community Church in Waco, Texas, for example, raise their own support. This is part of the process of walking by faith. I'm told that it normally takes six to eight months for ACC church planters to raise the money. Some actually like it! One ACC church planter who had recently gone on staff salary at the mother church said to me, "I miss the exciting walk of faith to have to depend on God for my monthly support."

Many church planters will raise support for a two or three year period. After that time they expect the church plant will be able to support them.

Often denominations will provide two to three years of support for their church planters. After that time period, the support will be incrementally withdrawn. If the church planter and the new church have not been able to gather enough people who have become Christ-followers to support the church planter through offerings, he will have to find a job in the community, which is often a blessing in disguise because it helps the church planter connect with the community.

Bi-vocational pastoring

Frequently church planters are bivocational. This is one of the major ways of cutting the costs of new church development. Peter Wagner writes, "Most growing denominations make good use of bivocational workers. They nurture these works by giving them special recognition, providing them services they need"[8]

If you plan on working as a bivocational "tentmaker," be sure to evaluate your energy level. A person who is a high extrovert may be able to handle a people-intensive job and still have enough energy to invest in the church plant. An introvert might be exhausted by too much time with people. A key principle is for your secular employment to compliment your church planting ministry. It should not deplete your emotional strength.

Some find energy in owning their own business, while others find this kind of activity to drain their creativity. Church planters must decide what will work best in their setting, in their family situation, and with their personality and abilities. Here are some options:

- Worship leader for another church
- Computer consultant/business
- Chaplain for businesses
- Construction/painting business
- Ministry role with district or region
- Accountant
- Sales in various areas
- Interim pastoral ministry with limited responsibilities
- Teaching at a local community college or Christian college

While some church planters see getting a second job as a necessary evil, others see it as an advantage because it keeps them more in touch with the very people they want to reach.

Determine the method

When planting new trees, nurseries are careful to properly fertilize the soil to allow the roots to grow properly. Those who plant trees know the dangers of growing a tree in one place and then planting somewhere else.

Churches often start in the womb of a mother church and are then birthed in another location. At other times the church only exists in the mind and heart of the church planter who moves to a new location to start the church.

Methods of church planting, in fact, are numerous. Some experts identify thirty distinct ways to plant a church (see appendix two). Two, however, stand out: Mother-daughter and Missionary approach.

Mother-daughter strategy

The mother-daughter model occurs when the host congregation commissions a group of people from the church to be the core group for a new church plant.

The core should be composed of people who have a "pioneer" mentality and are ready to settle somewhere else. Those who want to worship in the style they are used to in the mother church or who want things done "the normal way" are not good candidates for the church planting core group.

The core should be composed of people who have a "pioneer" mentality and are ready to settle somewhere else.

The new group should include people with diverse gifts who can serve the church in different ways. The core develops the vision, mission, and values for the new church. Ideally the lead church planter will come from the mother church and nurture the core within the mother church. Sometimes the core determines how they will call pastoral leadership (e.g., bi-vocational pastor or a lay minister). Sometimes a core member will provide pastoral leadership until the group feels ready to call someone fulltime.

Get a firm, permanent commitment from core members to join the daughter church plant. A permanent commitment avoids the leadership vacuum that occurs in new congregations when some in the group decide to return to the mother church. Breaking away from the home congregation allows the daughter church to establish its own identity and not become a clone of the mother church.

My second church plant was a mother-daughter one. We carried the core values from the mother church, as well as 150 people in ten cell groups. A committee from the mother church provided prayer, resources, and people. The mother church gave us liberty to become our own independent group, even though we gladly maintained the close relationship.

Missionary approach

The missionary approach may well be the oldest form of starting new congregations. In Acts 13:1-3, we read that the church at Antioch, prompted by the Holy Spirit, commissioned Paul and Barnabas for the ministry of spreading the gospel, beginning first in Cyprus.

The missionary approach takes place when the church planter raises up leaders from the harvest, rather than gathering a core from the mother church. Paul the apostle used this methodology as he planted churches throughout the then known world.

I've also tried the missionary approach to church planting on two different occasions and in chapters seven through nine of this book, I go into detail about how to plant a church from the ground up, using the missionary approach.

Find a coach

It can be painful and emotionally demanding to step out into the unknown and raise up a church. The pain and frustration can seem overwhelming at times. Failure knocks often at the church planter's door. And statistics are no consolation here. Many church plants shut down. Statistical reality, however, only emphasizes the need for coaching in the church planting process.

Coaching is critical in the life of a church planter. Great coaches practice:

- **Listening:** More than anything else, church planters need a coach who is willing to listen to their problems, fears, and needs.
- **Encouragement:** Church planters need encouragement and happily receive it at every opportunity. Great coaches continually

encourage church planters, acknowledging their important effort and ministry.

- **Care:** One difference between coaching and consulting is the relational element. The best coaches extol friendship and caring relationships. They demonstrate care by many practical gestures of love and kindness.
- **Development:** Often church planters hit empty. They run dry. Effective coaches help fill up the tank by supplying the pastor with resources: web articles, free books, and wise counsel that will help the planter become more effective.
- **Strategizing:** The goal of church planting is planting new churches. Coaches help the planter identify new pastors from among the existing small group leaders.
- **Challenging:** Coaches should never allow the leader to be content with mediocrity. *Care-fronting* means speaking the truth in love with improvement as the goal.
- **Receiving.** Great coaches receive daily food from Jesus from their personal quiet time. They're filled with the Spirit and then model what they've received from the Master.[*]

According to the statistics, many church planters quit. This should and can be prevented in many planting endeavors. Coaches can help church planters keep on course and not give up. Coaches have perspective and insight at another level. They perceived the diamond, even when the planter only sees the rough stone.

I will eventually cut down the dead tree next to my house. While it stands, however, I'm constantly reminded of how important roots are to a tree's health.

There are no shortcuts to planting a healthy, growing church. Trees grow large because they've grown deep. And every tree grower knows that growing roots takes a long, long time.

---

[*] **My book How to be a Great Cell Group Coach goes into detail about each of these aspects of coaching. For more information go to:** www.joelcomiskeygroup.com

Churches with no roots might appear beautiful for a time—and might even be the envy of the church planting circuit— but they are not equipped to last.

Make sure your church plant is equipped to last. Take the time to develop the roots. Go deep and you will grow tall.

Chapter Six

Aiming Accurately

Shooting guns is a guy thing. In 2002 my friend, Steve Fitch, invited me to go shooting in the badlands, a desert area between Moreno Valley and Beaumont, California. Seven men packed into their cars for a redneck time of shooting and hanging out. As the day wore on, it became apparent that the other men were much better shooters than I.

They shattered the clay pigeon discs that were flung into the air forty to fifty percent of the time. I only hit one or two discs—about a two percent ratio.

The problem was simple. My aim was way off.

My friends knew how to aim the gun slightly above the target to hit the disc in midair. Experience had also taught them how to brace themselves for the gun's recoil. I, on the other hand, had little knowledge or experience with shot trajectory. I rarely hit the flying disc.

When planting a church, it's essential to aim accurately. Without the right aim, church planting often resembles shooting at a flock of high flying geese blind folded. Not much chance that anything significant will take place.

So what can a church planter do to improve his or her aim?

Learning the customs and culture

When I took Peter Wagner's church planting course at Fuller Seminary in 1984, we spent several days discussing how to collect facts and statistics about our target audience. I had just begun planting Hope Alliance in Long Beach, California, so I visited the Long Beach library and spent several days collecting demographic information. I even contacted the Long Beach City Planning Department to purchase architectural maps that would give me critical information about the city of Long Beach.

Fast forward twenty years. Today, the same information can be collected at the click of a mouse. What I labored weeks and months to obtain in 1984 can now be gathered on the internet.

For example, by placing my zip code in a Google search, I can discover more information than I could ever need about race, ancestry, education, income, social status, population, lifestyle, and more. I can expand my search to include other zip codes of connecting cities. More information than a church planter could ever use is available online.

Like missionaries who spend years getting to know the language and culture of the target group, church planters must learn the distinct characteristics and cultural norms of the people they are trying to reach.

Yet, there's no substitute for the information that comes from spending time with the target audience. The Open Bible church planting movement states:

> When we work with planters, we try to bring them back to basic missiological principles and develop an appropriate model from there. Practically, this may mean the planter spends the first six months living among the people group learning everything he or she can about them. During this time, particularly if he or she is new to the area, the planter looks for the networks of relationships that exist within the community. He or she discovers who the influencers in those networks are. Then that pastor builds bridges into the lives of those influencers by using what they have in common as a starting point.[1]

As you spend time with people in your community, write down what you find and experience. I recommend that you compile all the material about your target group into a document that becomes your church case study.

The case study should include demographic material, personal observations about the target audience, church vision and values—anything meaningful for the church plant.

I've been adding material to my Wellspring case study for the last five years. It's grown to approximately 140 pages. I try to skim through the case study each day (or at least look at the table of contents) to keep the vision burning in my mind and heart and especially to bathe it in prayer.

Like missionaries who spend years getting to know the language and culture of the target group, church planters must learn the distinct characteristics and cultural norms of the people they are trying to reach. Whether the missionary is laboring in America or Timbuktu, understanding the culture is essential.

Reaching the people

My limited shooting experience involved a borrowed shotgun and flying clay pigeons. Those who win Olympic gold medals are those who spend lots of time shooting at the range—perfecting their aim through practice. The range for the church planter is where the people are. Inherent in the task of making disciples is spending time with those who are not yet Christ's followers. Ralph Neighbour writes:

> Reading and going to conferences and being mentored by another successful pastor does not grow a church. Growing a church is in direct proportion to how many hell raisers know I am a pastor who cares and associates with winebibbers. Quit reading and going to conferences and hanging around with successful pastors. Visit the 10 bars closest to where you live and make one friend in each. Then ask to meet the wife, etc., and drop by for coffee. We must declare war on a lifetime of being programmed to think Christian ministry can be done without making many friends among the gold plated hell raisers around us.[2]

Developing friendships

I consider some church planters exceptional in reaching the unchurched. One church planter I've had the privilege of coaching for the last several years is Jeff French, pastor of Resurgent church, a new church plant in Newnan, Georgia.

Jeff began his ministry by devouring books and articles on church planting. After determining his philosophy of ministry (a simple core to crowd approach), he visited growing churches that were multiplying small groups. He then found a coach to help him in the process. Jeff raised support for three years, so he could concentrate on the church plant. Thankfully, Laura, his wife teaches English fulltime at a local high school. Not only has it provided additional income, but it has been a breeding ground for getting to know people.

Jeff knew they had to find other ways to get involved in the community, so he tried several different approaches. One that has been effective is to go and play trivia at local sports bars and restaurants.[3] It has allowed Jeff and Laura to spend more time with people and get to know them.

Most of the people Jeff and Laura are making friends with don't talk about religion; even fewer go to church. Jeff doesn't force it. "Most of the people at the bar behave like grown up frat boys," Jeff told me. "They live to party." Yet, he's also noticed a lot of receptivity to Jesus outside the church.

When they ask Jeff what he's doing in the community, he plainly shares, "I moved here to start a church." Sometimes that takes people by surprise, but the relationships that have been built allow Jeff to relate to them personally rather than as just "some pastor." One guy responded to hearing about starting a church, "I was part of something like that in Savannah." His wife chimed in, "We need to get involved in something. We'd like to be in one of your groups."

Jeff found the first five couples to start his initial pilot group "on the range," by hanging out with people in the community.

One couple who joined the pilot group was Jeff's neighbor. Jeff entered their world by fixing things in their house. Eventually, the husband pulled Jeff aside and confessed marital struggles. Jeff listened and shared his own personal story. Jeff said to me, "A lot of people have struggles in marriage, but they just don't talk about it."

One of Jeff's relational strategies is to ask unchurched people what TV shows they like to watch. After hearing their reply, he'll say, "let's watch that show together. Why don't you come over to my house and we'll hang out."

Another relational strategy has been through the sport of volleyball. Jeff plays a lot of competitive volleyball. He plays with up to twenty to forty different people during the week. One guy was cussing around him for several weeks. When he found out Jeff was a pastor, he felt embarrassed. Jeff said, "I want you to be yourself. Don't act differently because of me." Since that time people have come up to Jeff, wanting to talk about personal things. One of the volleyball guys said to him, "Jeff, I have a ton of respect for you because you're willing to hang out with us. I live in an apartment complex. Maybe we could start a Bible study together?"

Jeff's advice to church planters is, "Find some things you enjoy and then do those things around and with unbelievers. Do you like tennis? Use that as a tool to get to know people. Then become intentional in getting to know those who you are with." Jeff likes to play volleyball, and his wife, Laura, loves trivia. They would be doing these things anyway. They've simply made it a conscious choice to do them around non-Christians (see endnote to find out other strategies the Frenches have used to reach out).[4]

From the contacts with outsiders, Jeff started his first pilot group in October 2007. Jeff's pilot group meets on Sunday evening. But first, he sends each person a lesson on Monday, which has both Bible content, reflective questions, and prayer prompts. Then on Thursday, he sends out an MP3 audio message on the same topic. The length of the audio is normally about twenty minutes. Since each person has already reflected on the Bible theme and the questions, the audio reinforces what they've already received.[*] On Sunday evening when they come together for the pilot group, each person is ready. Jeff combines group time together with smaller break-out groups.

---

[*]**Jeff sends out these MP3 messages and lessons via email as a free resource to anyone who requests them. Write to Jeff French at resurgentchurch@yahoo.com, and he'll place you on the list.**

Another relational evangelism hero of mine is Steve Irvin, who planted a church in Bogota, Colombia. When I first entered the door of Steve and Claudia Irvin's apartment in 2000, the living room was filled with non-Christians learning English (an outreach tool). I politely greeted them, excused myself, and unpacked my clothes for a weeklong stay.

The next morning, Steve knocked on my bedroom door at 7 a.m., informing me that he had plans to play golf with a non-Christian friend. "I hope to win this upper-class business person to Christ," Steve said. "At this point, he won't darken the door of a church." While eating breakfast that morning with the Irvins, the doorbell chimed and in stepped a non-Christian housewife from the same apartment complex. After introducing us, Claudia said, "We're going to go for a walk around the neighborhood. I'll be home later."

The next day, Steve and Claudia left the house early because they were going to exercise in the local gym. Why? To meet non-Christians. Two days later, the house was once again filled with non-Christians learning English. On my last day, Steve arrived home late because he was playing basketball with non-Christian friends.

"Okay, Lord," I thought. "What do you want to teach me through these choice servants?" Even though I had read most of the material on friendship evangelism, I had never seen such commitment and diligence in actively pursuing non-Christian relationships.

The Irvins have learned that most people must first be won through friendship before they attend a church. Their simple church plant has grown as a result of the friendship approach.

The Oasis Church in Bogotá, Colombia was started in 1996 by befriending non-Christians and then inviting them to a cell group that eventually multiplied. The church multiplied to twelve groups, and those groups came together on Sunday morning to worship Jesus Christ and study the word. Evangelism and harvesting primarily takes place within the home groups. And from the beginning, they've used friendship evangelism as the primary outreach tool.

Claudia, for example, began attending an aerobics class in her community in 1994. After aerobics, she stayed for coffee and began to develop relationships with the women.

Claudia eventually invited a few women from the exercise class to her house for informal teas. As friendships blossomed, some of the women would invite Claudia over to their houses for a cup of coffee and to talk about spiritual things. From there, an evangelistic Bible study was formed. Many of those ladies prayed to receive Christ there. Some of those original contacts participated in the first cell groups at the Oasis Church.

Steve told me that an important value at the Oasis Church is to avoid church busyness that hinders members from reaching non-Christians. "We don't want to become too churchy," Steve reiterated on several occasions.

My stay with the Irvins reminded me of what Jesus said: "It is not the healthy who need a doctor, but the sick. . . for I have not come to call the righteous, but sinners to repentance" (Matthew 9:12-13). The Oasis church is following the Master who was known as a friend of sinners.

Making a certain number of contacts

Many church planters don't naturally gravitate to non-believers. Instead, they need a plan to get them out in the community, interacting with non-Christians. Bill Mallick, a specialist in church planting, counsels church planters to make twenty contacts, or conversations, per week.[5] These might be conversations at Starbucks, a soccer game or a barbeque on the block. This does not mean the church planter will be sharing the gospel or "witnessing." Rather, the goal is to get out in the community and develop relationships.

Rob Campbell developed the "10-5-1 plan" to get church planters out in the community. The goal is to meet ten new people each week: the young woman who served coffee, the attendant at the gas station, the mail carrier, etc. The "who" doesn't matter. The key is that contact is made.

Beyond initial contact, the goal is to get the name of the person. Then the planter writes down the name and a reminder of what happened. Why? For prayer. Bathe the person in prayer, asking God's blessing and work in his or her life.

From the ten new contacts, the goal is to have a longer conversation with five each week. Conversational questions might include "What do you do for fun when you're not working?" or "When I met you yesterday, you were going to do this . . . how did that go?"

The strategy is to open up the lines of communication. Listening is key, while continuing to pray.

From the ten individuals, the goal would be to invite one person to the small group (or to the celebration service, if the church has them).

The invitation doesn't need to be given immediately. The planter might choose to wait to invite the person to a holiday outreach or small group dinner. The key is to realize that forming friendships and relationships are what church planters do. They spend time on the range. Rob writes:

> There's no hook or catch affixed to the 10-5-1 plan. God is in control. You are simply being used by Him to love and befriend others. Leave the results to Him. The 10-5-1 plan is a tool, not a rule. It's an intentional plan to keep you focused on the harvest. [6]

Rob realizes that a plan like 10-5-1 doesn't work for everyone. The bottom line, however, is that if church planters stay in their studies and don't get out into the community to mingle with pre-Christian people, the church will probably not grow. And the planter won't be exemplifying the nature of Jesus who was a friend of sinners.

If the church planter is naturally out in the community on a regular basis, there's no need for such a plan. But for those planters who prefer having a clear-cut plan, the 10-5-1 plan is a great option.

Improving your aim

I don't get an emotional high by pulling the trigger of a gun. Why? Because the jolt from the gun hurts. And the kickback also negatively affects the aim. I had to learn how to adjust my aim in order to shoot more accurately.

Spending time with people is necessary. But certain types of people are more open to the gospel message than others. For example, divorce, hospitalization, or even positive events such as childbirth or marriage can add stress and make people open to the gospel message. Some of life's events are more intense than others, as the below chart indicates.[7]

Event	Stress Value	Event	Stress Value
Death of spouse	100	Son or daughter leaving home	29
Divorce	73	Trouble with the in-laws	29
Marital separation	65	Outstanding personal achievement	28
Jail term	63	Spouse begins or starts working	26
Death of a close family member	63	Starting or finishing school	26
Personal injury or illness	53	Change in living conditions	25
Marriage	50	Revision of personal habits	24
Fired from work	47	Trouble with boss	23
Marriage reconciliation	45	Change in work hours or conditions	20
Retirement	45	Change in residence	20
Health change in family member	44	Change in schools	20
Pregnancy	40	Change in recreational habits	19
Sexual difficulties	39	Change in church activities	19
Addition to the family	39	Change in social activities	18
Business readjustment	39	Mortgage or loan under $10,000	18
Change in financial status	38	Change in sleeping habits	16
Death of a close friend	37	Change in eating habits	15
Marital arguments	35	Change in number of family gatherings	15
Mortgage or loan over $10,000.00	31	Christmas season	12

The message that Jesus Christ came to give us abundant life is a welcome respite during stressful times.

The best places to reach unchurched, needy people are among those who are bankruptcy, entering a twelve-step program, or having some other struggle. Rarely will the satisfied and the comfortable respond to Jesus. David Garrison, author and expert on church planting movements, writes:

> Great social stability tends to lull people into a false sense of security. They forget that life is short and that one must prepare for eternity. This creates an obstacle for affluent Western Europe, Japan, and the United States where unparalleled economic health has fostered unparalleled malaise.[8]

God often allows people to feel uncomfortable through crisis. The reason I cried out to Jesus in my bedroom in 1973 was because of the depression I felt as I pondered my future. What was I going to do? Who was I going to hang out with? What was life all about? The crisis reached a boiling point, and I found myself calling out to Jesus.

The message that Jesus Christ came to give us abundant life is a welcome respite during stressful times.

I heard one church planter say that often we don't go down far enough in the rungs of society to strike gold. We don't go to people who live in crisis and know their need for God. We prefer to hang out with the strong, the confident, and the satisfied—but those people ultimately don't feel the need for God. Jesus has a heart for the broken and bruised. His ministry focused on the poor, the spiritually bankrupt, and those on the fringe of society. Scripture says:

> The blind and the lame came to him at the temple, and he healed them. But when the chief priests and the teachers of the law saw the wonderful things he did and the

children shouting in the temple area, "Hosanna to the Son of David," they were indignant (Matthew 21:14-15).

Those who want Jesus are often the blind, the lame, and the outcasts. In Moreno Valley, California, there is a mosaic of nationalities with varied income levels, education, and social status. We have naturally been reaching the white, middle class. Yet, we are also discovering that some in our white homogenous group are the least flexible and hungry for ministry. We've felt compelled to go to the street corners and invite all (especially the needy) to come to the banquet of the King. After all, Jesus said:

> The wedding banquet is ready, but those I invited did not deserve to come. Go to the street corners and invite to the banquet anyone you find. So the servants went out into the streets and gathered all the people they could find, both good and bad, and the wedding hall was filled with guests (Matthew 22:8-10).

Jesus gathered a motley crew of both blue collar (fishermen) and white collar (tax collector and a physician) to be a part of the original twelve. Not only did he interact with the woman at the well in Samaria, but he also gave the commission in Acts 1:8 to the apostles, who would be witnesses in Jerusalem, Judea, Samaria, and the uttermost parts of the world.

The person of peace

God is the One who guides us toward people of peace. He is preparing an audience that is ready to hear the Good News.

The sovereignty of God should bring hope to the church planter. God is preparing people. Our job is to find them. Jesus said:

> When you enter a house, first say, 'Peace to this house.' If a man of peace is there, your peace will rest on him; if not, it will return to you. Stay in that house, eating and drinking whatever they give you, for the worker deserves his wages. Do not move around from house to house (Luke 10:5-7).

A *person of peace* is someone who God has sovereignly prepared to receive the gospel before you arrive. The essence of church planting, in fact, is finding those who God has sovereignly prepared. God is the One who wants to establish churches more than we do, and He makes it happen. He often does this by opening the hearts of key people.

In the early church, God opened the heart of Cornelius to hear and respond to the gospel (Acts 10). God prepared Cornelius to receive the ministry of Peter. The same thing happened with the conversion of Lydia. Scripture says:

> One of those listening was a woman named Lydia, a dealer in purple cloth from the city of Thyatira, who was a worshiper of God. The Lord opened her heart to respond to Paul's message. When she and the members of her household were baptized, she invited us to her home. "If you consider me a believer in the Lord," she said, "come and stay at my house." And she persuaded us (Acts 16:14-15).

The same thing happened with the jailer in Philippi (Acts 16:31-34). God used an earthquake to awaken him to the gospel.

Church planters need to pray for key individuals. The *person of peace* may or may not be a believer initially, but is open to the work of the gospel and receptive to its message. I mentioned Dave earlier in this book. He was already a believer but was very interested in my vision of planting a simple, reproducing church. God opened his heart to respond to my invitation to join us. Since he taught elementary school in Moreno Valley, he had lots of contacts and was very influential. Our family was new to the area, and Dave helped us connect. Our new church plant was often trying to reach Dave's friends, while we were in the process of establishing our own.

The bridgehead

The most terrifying battle scene in the movie *Saving Private Ryan* is when the allied forces invaded Normandy, France, on June 6, 1944. Because of the bridgehead that was established through the

D-Day invasion, by the end of August, 1944, all of northern France was liberated, and the invading forces reorganized for the drive into Germany, where they eventually brought an end to the Nazi Reich.

A bridgehead is a position seized by advancing troops in enemy territory, which serves as a basis for further advances. Like the allied forces, all church planters need a starting point. They need a definable foothold, that can expand as more troops join the force. Paul and his team found an entry point, a bridgehead into Philippi. Often the bridgehead was the Jewish synagogue.[9] One of the reasons why Paul liked the synagogue so much was that the Jews already feared God, and many were Greeks who had access into the community. These God-fearing Greeks would then become a bridgehead into the community.

It's interesting that after finding the bridgehead in Philippi, they were thrown into prison after casting out the demon from the fortune teller. Paul expanded his bridgehead through prison ministry. Shenk writes:

> Every church planter should plan and be alert to the historical moment which God brings into the experience of the newly planted church. We should embrace that moment of opportunity when the gospel speaks to the community with relevance and power. Sometimes it takes many years of faithful ministry until the moment of opportunity becomes clear. The opportunity is not always a crisis. It may be an open door for quiet ministry, or the conversion of a person, that God uses to reveal the glory of the gospel to the whole community. [10]

In the simple church strategy, the homes of the members are a bridgehead into the community. These groups need to be evangelistic in nature, with members always inviting new people to be part of the group.

Jeff Boersma planted a simple, reproducible church from a single cell group. During the first year he formed a leadership launch team, trained the leaders, met weekly for cell life, held several retreats, and prepared them for the multiplication of the first group. However, his launch team failed to launch. One-by-one, they left the pilot group. The problem: they were not able to reach the harvest.

During the second year, Jeff began over again with his wife and three kids in a small group. In the meantime they continued to develop relationships with the community. They eventually extended an invitation to people with whom they had developed a relationship, and three families agreed to join. They grew to thirty people and gave birth to a second group. Jeff had finally established his bridgehead among the unchurched.

The third year, Jeff birthed his third group. He writes:

I have weekly and monthly contact with our sets of leaders and feel good about our apprenticing process. However, it has been a challenging beginning to start a church with an entirely unchurched group of people. I guess I've learned again that God's ways are not always my ways.

Jeff goes on to say:

We are still a mom-and-pop shop compared to most traditional church plants, claiming only about forty that identify themselves with our church. Of course, that is eight times the size we were two years ago- when we were my family of five. It has been three years of persevering, forgiving a lot of hurt along the way, and sharing deeply in the joys, hurts, and lives of other people.[11]

Since my first shooting experience in the Badlands in 2002, I've had other opportunities. I even invited my daughter on one occasion, and she showed a lot of potential. Some say that practice can change any shooting amateur into an expert.

As you learn about the audience, spend time with non-Christians, and establish a bridgehead, then you'll be well on your way to planting a vibrant congregation.

But how exactly will you start your new church? The next few chapters take us to the heart of simple church planting. We'll look at practical strategies for planting churches that reproduce.

Section Three

Strategies for Starting Simple Churches

Simple Cell Church Planting

One church planter started a home group and multiplied it several times. Yet, as I talked with him, he felt discouraged, saying, "I'm just not sure if I'm the one who should lead this church plant." I just listened. He continued, "I should have more people by now so that I can launch this church."

"But you already have a church," I countered.

"But I need to have a lot more on the launch team to truly launch the church in the future," he replied.

Deeply ingrained in this church planter was the notion that his church really didn't exist until they had a major launch with many people. In the meantime, he was simply gathering people who were preparing to launch the real church. While he waited for the launch, he was weighted down with feelings of failure because others had told him that he should have more people in order to launch the church.

I counseled my friend to see his first cell as the church. I told him to enjoy the multiplication of individual cells, knowing that he had already planted the church. Eventually, he would bring those cells together in a celebration service to enhance all the believers through worship and teaching God's Word.

I wanted the church planter to feel the pure joy of knowing that he had already planted the church. Obviously his job was to steadily reach out, multiply cells, and continue to make disciples.

In many church planting approaches, small groups might be an important component in starting the church and even in continuing the church. However, ultimately the goal is to get the Sunday service going (or Saturday service). In the cell church strategy, the first cell group is officially the church. The goal is to multiply cells and bring them together to celebrate.

What is the cell model?

Most people know what a Sunday church service looks like. Worshippers gather to hear the word preached, worship the living God, and participate in the sacraments (e.g., the Lord's supper and baptism).

But what about the cell? The most common definition of a cell (and the one followed in this book) is: *a group of three to fifteen people who meet weekly outside the church building to practice evangelism, build community, and grow spiritually with the goal of multiplying the group.*

---

*The simplicity of cell church planting makes it exciting.
Even without a supporting mother church, a church planter
can open the first cell in a home and begin reaching non-
Christians.*

All small groups are not cell groups. One major difference between cell groups and other small groups is the cell's emphasis on evangelism, leadership development, and multiplication of each cell.

Cell churches also have other types of ministries (e.g., ushering, worship, prayer, missions, and training). These ministries, however, are not called *cell groups,* even though the particular ministry might be small and a group.[1]

In the cell church, the cell group is the backbone, or DNA of church ministry. Cell ministry replaces the need for many traditional programs.

I like to use the phrase *the cell-driven church* because the fruit is primarily measured through infrastructure growth as the church grows from the core to the crowd.

Some churches have cell groups as one of the programs in the church. In this scenario, the senior pastor, while overseeing all the programs, delegates the small group ministry to another person. In the cell church, however, the lead pastor is personally involved in cell ministry and is considered the point person and cell visionary. David Hesselgrave, professor emeritus of missions at Trinity Evangelical Divinity School, writes:

> The cell-celebration church has great appeal to postmodern young adults who are turned off by "impersonal" traditional churches and are longing for more intimate relationships and for shared leadership. Cell churches are uniquely positioned to reach the next generation for Christ because they are not about institutions and property but about living rooms and people. Related to this is a second benefit: this model has strong evangelism and discipling potential. Cell churches are focused on the harvest. Third, the rapid assimilation of new believers into the life of the church is enhanced by the cell group. Finally, the strong emphasis on training leaders to be able to train other leaders (every cell has both a coach and an apprentice) provides a constant pool of new lay workers for new outreach. Leadership and ministry are viewed as for everyone.[2]

Snapshot of cell church planting

The simplicity of cell church planting makes it exciting. Even without a supporting mother church, a church planter can open the first cell in a home and begin reaching non-Christians. The cell at this stage is more like a house church. The goal is to see non-Christians come to Christ, be trained through the training track, and then be sent out to lead their own cell group.

A church planter should form a team (there will be more on team development in the next chapter). The core team might come from the mother church, the denomination, a plea for "missionaries," help from another church, or even from among the unchurched.

The team meets together in a pilot cell for six months to one year. During that period, the core members of the pilot cell practice cell life, using the four Ws as a guide for the cell (see appendix three for more on the four Ws). Each core member is encouraged to get to know non-Christians in the neighborhood.

The church planter trains the core team members apart from the cell meeting.[3] In our church plant, we found it effective to set apart a Saturday or Sunday for concentrated training.

As the time gets closer for multiplication, the pilot group practices group evangelism, inviting new people to join one of the new groups. When the cell multiplies into several new cells, the church planter concentrates on coaching the new leaders while continuing to lead a regular cell group.

When there are four cells, begin monthly celebration services. Those monthly gatherings might take place in a park, a school, or church building. When there are approximately ten cells with 100 people, I recommend a weekly celebration service. A key part of the DNA from the very beginning is to plant new cell churches.

Return to simplicity

It is true that some cell churches are huge, yet most are small and flexible.[4] More and more leaders around the world are attracted to a simple form of church life, one that doesn't require huge budgets and super-talented preachers but follows the pattern of the New Testament church. I now find myself desiring a simple, reproducible, New Testament model.

Tomorrow's cell church won't depend on large buildings or technology to make it work. One reason the megachurches appear so complicated is that they are. One influential megachurch in the suburbs of Los Angeles, for example, is embarking on a ten-year expansion project with a 4000-seat worship center, an artificial lake, food court, coffee house, and recreational attractions including a rock-climbing wall and jumbo video screens.[5]

The beauty of a simple cell church is that it's reproducible.

A person who has led a cell, multiplied it, and coached the daughter cell leader has completed the core basics of cell church planting. Such a person is a prime candidate for future church planting—anywhere in the world.

Undoubtedly, a potential church planter will seek out biblical education and grow in the knowledge of Jesus Christ. Fruitfulness on the cell level builds confidence for future church planting and allows the candidate to then make it happen. The order is clear cut:

- Attend a cell.
- Receive training.
- Plant a cell.
- Multiply the cell several times.
- Coach the leaders who have multiplied into other groups.
- Receive more biblical training.
- Plant a church in the US or overseas using the same strategy.

Cell churches don't require a huge budget, a large plot of land, modern buildings, or super-talented pastors. The cell strategy uses the houses of people all over the city as the primary meeting locations. Instead of laboring to get people out of their houses once a week for an hour-long service, it seeks to utilize those same houses to reach an entire city and nation.

A peson who has led a cell, multiplied it, and coached the daughter cell leader has completed the core basics of cell church planting.

In May 2002 I spoke to denominational executives who were highly influenced by the house church movement. They resisted the idea of the megachurch because of the mega-problems associated with this phenomenon: mega-buildings, mega-land space, and bureaucratic nightmare of mega proportions.

I encouraged these leaders not to reject large cell churches altogether. "After all," I told them, "if God calls a pastor who can lead a cell church to megachurch status as a flagship church, such a church could have a powerful influence." Bethany World Prayer Center is one of those examples. Mega cell churches, however, shouldn't be the norm or the goal. The vast majority of cell church pastors will have smaller, more flexible churches that focus on church planting. Ralph Neighbour, an expert on cell church ministry writes:

> I have myself come to the conclusion that the combination of cell and megachurch is not the way to go and at present I am working on a model of a cell church that would form cells that would in turn create congregations of 50-60, but would still belong to a vision and a movement. I personally can envision planting a network of smaller cell churches across the city. I could envision these house churches being made up of 5-10 cells. Each cluster would meet monthly in celebration services (or twice per month) but weekly in cells. I can envision this type of church plant happening all over the world. It's not necessary to have a large cell church.[6]

Cell churches can give birth to new cell churches of any size. Some will grow large, but I sense a new wave of planting simple, reproducible cell churches.

Variations of cell church planting

Most cell churches give birth to daughter cell churches in the same city, as I've illustrated throughout this book. Some cell churches, however, choose to plant only one cell church per city. The Elim Church in San Salvador is an example of this strategy.[7] Elim does plant churches in different cities—just not in the same city. The Elim Church now has more than 120 churches in distinct cities around the world with about 200,000 attending them. Before Elim starts a celebration service in a city, they wait until there are at least five cell groups fully operating. They want to make sure the cell system is fully functioning before they go public.[8]

Other cell churches have chosen to plant satellite cell churches that are connected to the mother church. The finances of the satellite churches, for example, are administered through the mother church, and the satellite pastors are seen as staff pastors for the mother church. Often the satellite pastors attend the weekly staff meeting, with the exception of those staff pastors who live too far away. [9]

One caution: A senior pastor should never try to keep leaders under his control through the satellite model. Some satellite pastors may feel trapped and never able to fully express themselves as the pastor of their own church. We need to be willing to release anyone who wants to plant a church, and then do our best to assure the success of the new church.

My personal conviction is that few cell churches will ever grow to mega-cell church status and that church planting should be a higher priority than expanding one church.

Plant!

People ask me, "Joel, why are you so interested in cell church planting?" I tell them that cell groups are the perfect place to develop new leaders. Leaders are not developed and released by sitting in church on Sunday morning or worshipping in a large group. In a cell, a person can develop into a leader. Cell ministry brings out the ministry skills a person will need in a future church plant—pastoring, caring, counseling, evangelizing, and coaching. It's the perfect microcosm to prepare a mature, future church planter.

Reproduction is at the heart of the cell church movement. This reproduction comes at the level of cell multiplication, but it must move into the realm of church planting because church planting is the best way to fulfill the great commission of Jesus Christ.

I've painted the big picture for cell church planting. Now we need to look at the nuts and bolts of the planting process.

Chapter Eight

How to Plant a Cell Church

On February 13, 1988, Celyce and I were married by Dr. Harold Mangham. Before the wedding he gave us two pieces of advice. "First, learn to continually say *I'm sorry*. Second, find a couple who you can meet with regularly throughout life. This will help you to stay accountable."

We've tried to apply Dr. Mangham's advice throughout our marriage. Saying *sorry* and asking for forgiveness is something we try to practice constantly. And we do have one couple who we meet with regularly, Owen and Debby Schumacher. Owen was my best friend before I met Celyce. And Debby, Owen's girlfriend at the time, introduced me to Celyce. We are the same age, had children at about the same time, and have walked through life together for the last twenty years.

Owen and Debby are relief workers in Afghanistan, so it's hard to meet with them often. However, in June 2008 we had our ninth retreat together in Breckenridge, Colorado. We hadn't seen them in three years.

The first night we went out to eat at a Mexican restaurant. We then came back to the apartment to plan our time together. Our family of five and their family of six sat down for an old-fashioned business meeting. We laid out the possibilities that included hiking, going to a museum, ice-skating, feeding the chipmunks, spending time at the recreation center, and, of course, alone time for the adults. We voted on what we wanted to do and then arranged our plans for each day.

As the three days unfolded, we made numerous adjustments. We decided the second day, for example, that the recreation center was too expensive. We opted for the free "association pool" where we were staying. We also changed the ice-skating time from the second to the last day. Even though we changed our plans, we had a plan. We knew what we desired to do.

Plans are meant to be adjusted, but there's no reason not to have one. Church planters who make detailed plans are far more likely to succeed than those who fail to plan. Effective church planters change their plans as they listen to the Spirit of God, interact with the target audience, and discover what works best.

What are some of the key steps to plant a simple cell church?

First step: recruit a team of prayer warriors

When my wife and I first left for Ecuador in 1990 to plant churches, we somehow believed that by establishing many social relationships and eating lots of desserts with people, we had established a strong base. We faithfully wrote personalized letters to twenty-five churches each month, but the impact was minimal. When we returned for furlough, we realized that earlier friendships had faded. People moved on. Then I read C. Peter Wagner's book, *Prayer Shield*, and caught a new vision to gather intercessory prayer warriors to stand with me and my family. Gathering a team of committed prayer warriors has revolutionized our ministry.

In *Prayer Shield*, Wagner shows why intercessory prayer for Christian leaders is needed, as well as how to ask for it. I bought seventy-five copies of this book and handed it out to people who I recruited as prayer warriors. It was well-worth the money spent. Anyone planting a church will benefit from reading this book. Each team member needs to develop a prayer shield and form part of someone else's prayer shield.

The apostle Paul was a prayer recruiter. Paul wrote to the Colossian church, "And pray for us, too, that God may open a door for our message, so that we may proclaim the mystery of Christ, for which I am in chains. Pray that I may proclaim it clearly, as I should" (Colossians 4:3-4).

He said something similar to the church in Thessalonica, "Brothers, pray for us" (1 Thessalonians 5:25). Then to the church in Rome, Paul wrote, "Now I beseech you, brothers, through the Lord Jesus Christ, and through the love of the Spirit, that you strive with me in your prayers to God for me" (Romans 15:30). To the Corinthians, Paul said, "You also helping together in prayer for us, that thanks may be given by many persons on our behalf for the gift granted to us through many" (2 Corinthians 1:11).

Plans are meant to be adjusted, but there's no reason not to have one. Church planters who make detailed plans are far more likely to succeed than those who fail to plan.

Paul, the superb church planter, knew he couldn't make it without prayer. Do you know this?

Second step: develop values and vision

You'll know if God has called you to plant a cell-based church by your passion and conviction. Do you feel compelled to raise up leaders who multiply new groups? Do you love relational evangelism? Are you convinced of the need for community? As you read through the last chapter on starting a cell church, did you feel called to start a simple cell church?

Probably you've read some literature on cell church ministry. Read everything you can. There is a recommended reading list on my own site, www.joelcomiskeygroup.com. I encourage cell church planters to read through as many of the recommended books as possible.* One of the pastors I coached took a six-month sabbatical just to read and reflect on cell ministry. He was convinced that God had called him to plant a cell church but didn't know much about

---

* Reading list: http://www.joelcomiskeygroup.com/articles/churchLeaders/cellreadinglistbibliography.htm

it. He read and reflected on cell church literature, and we worked through key books together. Not everyone can take a sabbatical, but all church planters need to take time to learn the basics of cell ministry. This particular church planter looks back at his sabbatical as one of the best choices he made.

Visiting a cell church will also help you get a feel for the vision and values of cell ministry. The pastor who took the sabbatical also visited two dynamic American cell churches. In my book, *The Church That Multiplies,* I include forty-four cell churches I'd recommend in North America (there are many more).[**] In *Reap the Harvest,* I highlight many more worldwide cell churches.[***]

I would recommend that you attend a small group seminar to find out how to lead and multiply a small group.[****]

You must come to the place where you are ready to move beyond cell church models and discover key cell church principles on your own. I consulted one pastoral team who was constantly trying to copy the success of another churches. They bounced from trying to copy one successful church's format to another, never discovering their own philosophy of ministry. They had neglected the basic principles of cell church ministry and became entangled in duplicating the outward form of someone else's experience. Reading, visiting cell churches, and going to seminars will help you understand the heart of cell ministry—the key principles (see appendix four for a list of key cell church principles).

If at all possible, become involved in a cell church before trying to plant one. It's also important to lead a cell group and multiply it before trying to plant a cell church. Why? Because this is essentially what you'll be doing in the church plant. Bob Roberts, Jr. wisely counsels:

[**] **Church that Multiplies: http://store.joelcomiskeygroup.com/cech-sotrchin.html Or find them online: http://www.joelcomiskeygroup.com/articles/worldwide/worldwide.htm**

[***] **Reap the Harvest: http://store.joelcomiskeygroup.com/reha-howsmgrs.html**

[****] **Listing of my own seminar schedule: http://www.joelcomiskeygroup.com/speakingSchedule.htm**

The church planting interns start small groups in our church, so they are part of our normal, ongoing community. They get to "take with them" anyone they reach in their small group, keeping in mind that the majority of their people are going to come from outside Northwood. If they can't start a small group, why should they think they can start a church? If all they do is gather existing church members for their small group, they haven't indicated their ability to plant a church. When they gather people from outside Northwood, we start getting excited.[1]

Leading and multiplying a small group will give you confidence to do the same in a church planting setting. Simple church planting is all about raising up leaders for the harvest who can lead home groups and keep the process going.

Third step: invite people to the pilot cell group

The pilot group is your first cell group. When you start your pilot group, you have started your church. The first people in your pilot group are the charter members. They will be the foundation stones for the future.

The pilot group should not exceed fifteen adults. If it does, start two or more pilot groups at the same time.

Why start a pilot group? Because cell ministry is better "caught than taught." As the first leaders catch the vision for cell ministry, they will then impart what they've experienced to others. The core members will also get to see, feel, and interact with the values of the lead pastor.

Mistakes made in the pilot group stage are more easy to correct at the beginning. If the pilot group does not practice evangelism, neither will any of the resulting groups. If pilot group leaders do not model leadership development, neither will any of the resulting groups.

You can find people for your pilot group from friends, family, neighbors, a mother church, or co-workers. As mentioned earlier, the whole process of recruitment needs to be bathed in prayer. Through your prayers, God will guide you to the divine appointments—the people He has been sovereignly preparing.[2]

Places to find your core group

In Ecuador we were blessed to take 150 from the mother church, along with ten cell groups to start a daughter church five miles away.[3] At Wellspring we had no such advantage. We planted the church with my family and one other person.

So where do church planters find their initial group?

Jeff French is a great example of finding his pilot cell group from neighbors and friends he met at a bar and other places. Before starting a pilot cell, Jeff volunteered for a variety of activities with the hope of making contacts. People learned to love and appreciate him, and he was their friend. Soon a group formed from his contacts.

Through your prayers, God will guide you to the divine appointments—the people He has been sovereignly preparing.

Jeannette Buller promotes finding the people for the pilot group through the use of multiple "pre-cells" that are short-term. She writes:

> I would suggest starting with some short-term "pre-cells," which are focused on a particular need or interest in your ministry focus group. These could be evangelistically oriented Bible studies, instructional help such as finances or parenting, or simply an interest group on a specific topic. As the trust develops, you will be able to talk to them about joining something more permanent.[4]

Some have found it helpful to ask people for prayer requests. Sometimes God decides to miraculously answer the prayers, which in turn builds trust in the church planter and the church plant. Those who God has touched are willing to join the core group.

It sounds ideal to find all of the members of the pilot group from non-believers. Yet, it's also good to have some foundational members who know Jesus and have caught the cell vision. Aubrey Malphurs writes:

> The vision of the new church is not to steal sheep from the other churches (transfer growth), but to win sheep from the community (conversion growth). At the initial planting, however, the new church will need a group of mature believers as an important part of its foundation. This may involve some transfer growth initially.[5]

Ultimately, it's good to have a mixture of both believers and unchurched. Peter Wagner writes:

> I am aware that some recommend that when we start a new church. . . it is best to start with a group of unchurched people and develop them into a church. I can understand where they are coming from. They say that if we want new wineskins to contain the new wine, we do not need those who are dragging old wineskins around with them to get in the way. And this has worked in some instances. It is my opinion, however, that most church planters would do well to have a core of people around them who bring some of the technical skills that unchurched people would not have.[6]

One couple who joined our initial pilot group at Wellspring had moved from Long Beach to Moreno Valley. The wife had been involved in a cell church in the Philippines and was excited to get involved in what we were doing. This couple served as foundational members for the first two years of the church.[7]

Yet, some church planters find the core from among non-traditional Christians. One cell church planter wrote, "I know it sounds a little strange, but when starting new cell churches, I look for people who love Jesus tremendously, but who are sick of church."[8] Here in Moreno Valley we had a few people who were tired of church as usual and wanted to be involved on the ground floor of something new and exciting (note: they were not attending another church at the time).

Discerning the level of commitment among the core

It's not wise to accept people into your pilot group who are already committed to another evangelical church. You will face problems of conflicting authority and time commitments. Since the "other church" is where they worship and already have social relationships, they will be unwilling to commit themselves fully to the new church plant.

Those who have split loyalties will have a hard time accepting your church's overall vision.

Those who have split loyalties will have a hard time accepting your church's overall vision. Take outreach, for example. If a person has not yet committed to the church plant, most likely they will not be willing to evangelize and bring new people into the church, since they themselves are not committed. And even if they were to attract unchurched people, they would send out mixed signals about commitment to the local church, since their own loyalties are divided.

When it comes to serving, can they be counted on to be there and contribute to the larger goals? And what about financially supporting the new work? If a person is not committed to one church, it manifests itself in finances.

More importantly, cell church ministry is about making disciples in community. Community comes with bumps and bruises. You can't avoid times of real struggle as you accept the faults and failures of others. Like a marriage, it takes a real commitment to be there through good and hard times. It means saying, "We are a family, and we will stick this out until God changes us."

If a person is committed only half-way, when things get difficult, they will go somewhere else.

My recommendation is to allow the person to test your cell for a short while (perhaps a month or two). Then simply ask the person to make a decision. Try to do it as gently as possible, knowing that it's perfectly OK if the person decides to leave and minister elsewhere.

Many cell church planters have their pilot group meeting on Sunday evening. This is a good choice because people are accustomed to viewing Sunday as "church day." Meeting on Sunday evening sends the message that the pilot cell is the church.

We also had our first training events on Sunday morning, partly to send the message that we were truly a church from the very beginning and expected people to commit to our pilot cell as their church.

In the initial stages of a cell church plant, there won't be a full-blown Sunday worship service. It is not a problem if someone wants to attend a Sunday service somewhere for a more complete experience of worship and teaching. I do make sure the person is primarily connected to our church, both with their time and financial commitment.

Find your key leaders

Jesus chose his twelve disciples from among the multitude and then He selected three to enter into a closer relationship with Him. Those three were part of Christ's inner circle.

We felt led to do something similar among those in our pilot group at Wellspring. We discovered that not all pilot group members were equally committed. Some stood out. We had one couple, for example, who could never clearly tell us if they were fully committed to our church plant. They attended the celebration service at a church in a neighboring city and weren't sure about their commitment. They wanted to "see what was going to happen with our church" before they made their commitment.

We realized that this couple would not be part of our leadership team. Yet, we didn't exclude them, since they were with us from the beginning. So we made a list of requirements for those who chose to form part of the initial leadership team.

Requirements/Commitments: top leadership at Wellspring

Commitment to make Wellspring the main local church:
- Commitment to the vision of Wellspring.
- Commitment see pastor Joel Comiskey as the primary pastor.
- Commitment to see Wellspring as their church.[9]

Commitment of time:
- Commitment to be at all planned training events.
- Commitment to Wellspring--just as a person commits to be at their job every day, so also a person should be commit to be at Wellspring.

Commitment of tithe:
- Agree that 10 percent or more of gross income should be given to the Lord.
- Agree to give the majority of that ten percent to Wellspring.

Commitment to eventually lead a cell group.
Commitment of purity and holiness.
Commitment to maintain a regular, consistent devotional time.

The couple in question was not willing to make a deeper commitment and became attendees of our initial cell group, rather than part of the key leadership core.

Give yourself enough time in forming the pilot group

Ralph Neighbour writes, "In answer to the question about how a cell church plant finds its core group, here in Houston for me it has been v-e-r-y s-l-o-w-l-y!"[10] My experience is that a true pilot group takes time to gel.

Some will come, check out the group, and decide it's not a right fit. Some will not want to commit the time to join a church at the beginning. Others will be critical of the lack of normal church programs and activities. Some won't feel comfortable with those present. One experienced church planter, wrote:

I have found that in some cases the core comes together fairly rapidly. In most cases so far, though, it takes time. In one case, I went an entire year with just one family. When God finally moved, it was an awesome thing to watch. The trick is to stay faithful in prayer and watching. Henry Blackaby says we should watch to see where God is working and seek to join Him. I say it a little differently. I am looking for the footprint of God and trying to step in it. The hard part, though, comes when I haven't seen a footprint in a while. The temptation is to make one for Him, but it's the wrong thing to do![11]

Trying to find new ways to invite people is part of the process of growing the church. It's easy to underestimate the struggles and loneliness. The bottom line is that church planting takes time.

What to do in the pilot group?

Lead your pilot cell like a normal cell group. It's important to exemplify from the very beginning what you plan the future cell groups to follow. The values and vision you establish in the first cell will reverberate to all the future cell groups. I included in appendix three a normal cell group order, using the 4Ws, along with a sample lesson to follow.

Train future leaders

Training is in addition to the modeling that will take place in the pilot group. Training those in the pilot group can be done either before or after the cell group or on a different day. In the beginning stages of Wellspring, we used Sunday morning to do training.

Most cell churches have developed a training track, and they ask all their people to go through it. I've written about training tracks in cell churches in my book, *Leadership Explosion*.[12]

What kind of materials should be used for training? Great materials are available today. I've developed a five-book equipping series that is available for purchase. Look at what someone else has developed as a template for your own training track.[*] On my website, there are helpful articles about how other cell churches design their equipping series.[**]

Fourth step: multiply pilot group

When you have trained future leaders and have between ten and fifteen in your pilot group, it's time to multiply into at least two cells. Determine who will go into each cell group. Plan the date for multiplication with the group itself.

After multiplication, your new role as church planter will be to coach the new leaders as well as lead one of the cell groups.[13] As coach of the new leaders, you will visit their groups and meet with the leaders on a one-on-one basis.[***]

Leading your own group while coaching others will remind you of the importance of developing relationships with unchurched people—an absolute necessity in effectively planting a cell-based church.

Rob Reimer, church planter in New England, exemplifies the evangelism fervor he wants others to follow. He writes, "I'm passionate about reaching lost people, and I preach it and model it. If the senior pastor doesn't preach it, bleed it, and model it, people won't listen to what he says, and do what he does! He has to lead the way."[14] Reimer likes his groups to multiply only after they have reached two new people for Christ. The church planter's role is critical in maintaining the evangelistic focus.

---

[*] Visit http://store.joelcomiskeygroup.com/fiboeqse.html to see my five-book equipping series.

[**] Visit http://www.joelcomiskeygroup.com/articles/training/cell-Training.htm for additional articles on training.

[***] Read How to be an Effective Cell Group Coach- http://store.joelcomiskeygroup.com/howtobegrceg.html

---

Advice for multiplying a group[15]

Prenatal (weeks #1, 2 and 3)
- Have new leader, host, and a few members selected who will start the new group.
- Talk about the upcoming birth and why it is important.
- Divide the group for ministry time. Have the new team go to different parts of the house.
- It is important that the new team develops social relationships during the week (phone calls, social contacts, etc.).

Birth (week #4)
- Meet as separate cells but in the same house.

Postnatal (weeks #5-12)
- Meet as two separate cells in two different locations (weeks #5, 6 and 7)
- Meet back together for a reunion. This should not be a formal meeting but a time of fellowship and enjoying one another (Week #8 - one month after birth)
- Meet as two separate cells in two different locations (Week #9, 10, and 11)
- Meet back together for a reunion. Generally by this time cell members enjoy being together but find they have made the transition and their new cell is really where they are connected! (Week #12 - two months after birth)

Fifth step: start celebration worship

Just like a new birth that begins in the womb and results in a fully formed child, the cell church strategy starts behind the scenes and grows into a public demonstration of what's already happening. Bill Beckham writes:

One method of beginning a cell church is the popular but flawed "big bang" theory. In the "big bang" theory a cell church develops out of a cataclysmic event by which the church appears complete and fully formed. The theory is the opposite of the process principle Jesus used to build the first church. Church leaders, especially pastors of large churches, are attracted to the "big bang" theory because it seems to eliminate much of the pain and the patience required in a step-by-step process. It promises to give instant gratification to vision. However, the "big bang" theory is a fatal attraction. It weakens the learning process of leaders and compromises the developing process necessary to strengthen the infrastructure. [16]

In the cell church strategy, the church has already begun through the cell. The essence of the celebration is connecting the cells together. The celebration services causes each person in the church to see themselves as part of a greater whole.

Many cell church planters start celebration services too early and get trapped placing too much energy into a celebration service, losing the cell focus and momentum. Bob Logan and Jeannette Buller write:

> Most traditional church plants begin with a full-blown public worship with as many buzzers and bells as can be mustered. Much time and energy goes into preparing for this service, including various forms of advertising and, often, borrowed leadership to pull it off. Because cell-celebration churches want to put their emphasis on reaching unchurched people and participating in life-transforming cell groups, the worship service is not usually a primary focus in the initial stages of the church plant. [17]

The importance of waiting

Granted, it's very hard to wait to start celebration services because church culture still expects a Sunday morning gathering. I personally started the celebration service too soon in my first church plant in Long Beach, California in 1983. Everything went well in the beginning when the church met in my home. The house church grew and prospered. The time came to multiply to an additional home group and my original plan was to start various cells that would then meet once per month together on Sunday night.

One key couple, however, resisted my plan. They wanted to meet every week in a celebration gathering. At the time, I had not established my own philosophy of ministry. I was tossed back and forth by every wind of church growth theory. To please this couple, I decided to have a weekly celebration for everyone who wanted to be involved. We started meeting on Sunday morning. I hoped to keep the home groups alive, but soon found that all my time and attention were going to the weekly celebration—just trying to get people to attend that service. It was an exhausting experience, and I don't recommend it.

Launching a celebration service too early is a common problem. When a few people come together in such a situation, it feels like eating at a bad restaurant. The lack of people seems to indicate the food is bad. Jason Hoag, a church planter in Florida, said:

> We have started a cell church (or what we thought was a cell church) in April 2000 in Orlando, Florida. The leadership team and I are realizing now that in our ignorance, we started with a big meeting (boy do I wish we could do that one over again).[18]

I gave a seminar to Southern Baptists in Florida and discovered that most of the church planters started their church with a celebration service. When I spoke about the need to first multiply the pilot group and to grow the infrastructure naturally before starting the celebration, most of them nodded in agreement. They knew firsthand the difficulties of trying to celebrate with so few people. They regretted that their celebration service felt more like a cell group than a true Sunday service.

Keith Bates, a church planter in Australia, writes: "I think now I would probably have just run cells and not had a bigger meeting for a while. That would have said that this church is radically different." Like a lot of church planters, Keith Bates probably thought that a weekly celebration would give him more people, but, in reality, it doesn't. It often hinders church growth because people don't get a true sense of celebration.

Resist the temptation to begin regular celebration services before establishing the infrastructure of the cell groups. Otherwise, it puts too much strain on too few people.

Dean Dequera, a former church planter in the San Francisco area, writes:

Although we take full responsibility for the failed attempt, there were a lot of factors that led to our failure. We basically found ourselves in a crowd to core approach instead of a core to crowd. Then we were stuck trying to teach "old dogs new tricks." Values take time to develop and we must resist the pressure to produce a crowd overnight in order to help us survive financially. [19]

Dean, a good friend of mine, found himself having to produce a quick crowd with no foundation. He faced the church planter's dilemma—produce or perish. The instant crowd approach created a false dichotomy and put too much strain on the church.[20] Lyle Schaller writes:

If the mission developer yields to those pressures to begin corporate worship soon after arrival, that often means beginning with a smaller number and diverting much of that church planter's time and energy away from cultivating new constituents.[21]

When to go public

Small groups are supposed to be small. Large rooms, however, with few people lack vibrancy, and a certain emptiness engulfs everyone. A study from *Leadership Journal* a few years ago found that the average size for starting a church was forty-three.[22] Increasingly, however, church leaders have recognized the need to have even more people to start a viable *weekly* celebration service. A blurb on the Disciples of Christ website encouraged their church planters to start weekly worship services when there were 100 people involved in the core group.

I think it's best to wait until there are 100 people in approximately ten cell groups before committing to a weekly celebration service. Until then, it's normal and acceptable for the cells to meet once per month in a celebration service or once every two weeks.[23] Many cell church plants also fulfill the need for the larger gathering with half-night prayer meetings and social gatherings.

Waiting for approximately 100 people before weekly celebration assures that the same people won't be doing the same Sunday ministries over and over. It's also essential not to depend on a few key families to show up each celebration time in order to have enough people to truly celebrate. With 100 people in the cell groups, some families can miss the celebration, and most likely the key celebration functions will continue as planned (e.g., children's church, worship team, and so forth).

Several years ago, two church planters started pioneering a cell-based approach at River Rock Church in Folsom, California. They worked hard to build cells, develop leaders, enter into the life of the community, and build infrastructure for the church. All that required great patience, persistence, keeping faith with their vision, and delaying the grand opening.

When they had their first public service, they were ready. The infrastructure was in place. They had eight cell groups with leaders, apprentices and several experienced members, ministry teams, a leadership team, a web site, and a clear vision for their church.

Most importantly, members were inviting people. The church has grown rapidly in both cell and celebration. People who came to their first celebration service saw something alive, exciting, authentic, and worth coming back to.[24]

Key Question: do you need weekly celebrations?

The cells of a cell church should meet together in a large group gathering. Not all cell churches, however, meet *weekly* in corporate gatherings. Cell churches, in other words, do *not* need to gather together weekly in corporate worship to be called a cell church. Weekly celebration services will not be the norm for every church.

I don't think that the definition of a cell church requires a weekly celebration meeting. Rather, I believe that the cells do need to gather together in corporate worship to be called a cell church. The frequency of that meeting is what's in question. The great benefit of the weekly celebration is that the cell church can reach out more frequently through the celebration wing. Yet, the cell must drive the church. The main priority is for the cells to meet weekly. Those cells should be networked together through pastoral care, coaching, training, and coming together. And these are the things that define a cell church—not whether the celebration meets weekly or not. I asked Bill Beckham about this, and he wrote back saying:

> It seems to me that large group celebration can be very flexible in terms of frequency, place, number of people involved and even format of the meeting. Celebration was certainly flexible in the New Testament. Of course we must answer a question about the reference in the New Testament to "the first day of the week." What were they doing on the "First Day of the Week?" Were they meeting every "First Day" of the week in a large group expression? Or, were they meeting weekly in small group expression and from time to time in large group expression. I am inclined to believe that it is the second suggestion. I believe that we must operate from the large group celebration principle and not from the historical precedent of a large group meeting. The Body of Christ needs to experience God in a large group expression along with the small group and house church expression. I believe the 21st Century Church is finding innovative ways to live out the principle.[25]

The cell church movement needs to develop new models of how the church will function in its large group expression. And we must remember that the large group expression is not just the time of public worship. In addition to public worship, the large group expression could be used for training, for showing a public face in the city, for fellowship, for coordination, and for evangelism. Lon Vining writes:

> The church I helped plant in Boulder, Colorado, called Quest has now gone to once-a-month services, and the other three Sundays they hang out with their cell groups and bring along lost friends. They have programmed in enough free time in which they can actually spend time with each other and with lost persons, making friendships. Statistics and experience have borne out that that's really the place Christ is introduced to a non-believer—through deep, committed friendships. When

we know these two facts, then to throw all of our eggs in the relationship building basket makes complete sense, and doing anything that takes a lot of time and energy that does not build our cell or our outside relationships does not make much sense.[26]

I coach some cell church planters who never want weekly celebrations. And that's okay. And then some pastors can't manage both a weekly cell structure and weekly celebration.

The cells of a cell church should meet together in a large group gathering. Not all cell churches, however, meet weekly in corperate gatherings.

The focus should remain on the weekly cells, and the celebration should develop as the cells build strength. Those cells might celebrate all together on a weekly basis or a monthly basis. Or they might meet together more than once per week, like in the case of Elim.[27] They might even meet once a quarter.

Finding a location for the celebration service

Most church planters recommend renting property to start a church.[28] I would suggest that churches save money and rent facilities. Meeting in a rented facility means developing a "portable approach" to ministry. There are various choices:

- Many churches use another church's facility.
- School rentals are another great option, because they are neutral places. In my first church plant, we rented at an elementary school for several years. Today school rental can be a very expensive option.
- Day care sites are another option.
- Community centers hold promise for many church plants.

- Restaurants and meeting halls (legion hall) are great choices for many.
- Fire stations often provide great meeting places.
- Hotels are the choice of many. Wagner says, "I feel that one greatly underutilized space in many of our communities are hotel or motel conference rooms. These are often full during the week but empty on weekends. Hotel sales managers would like to keep them full seven days a week. The prices on these rooms are in most cases highly negotiable."[29] In my current church plant, we are meeting at a Best Western Hotel in Moreno Valley.

People do get tired of needing to set up church for each celebration, so the pastor needs to diligently cast the vision and delegate responsibilities to a wide variety of people.

Sixth step: build the infrastructure

After the cells have multiplied and you're able to bring them together to celebrate, it's now time to work on the coaching structure, perfect the equipping track, and develop other components of the cell church such as the cell reporting system. *****

I always encourage the pastor to continue to lead a cell or be part of a cell leadership team. Personal involvement allows the pastor to freely add cell examples to sermons. A pastor who is personally involved in a cell can speak from personal experience about the need for community, body-life evangelism, leadership development, and the use of the gifts of the Spirit.

The coaching structure should stay strong on two levels. The first level is the senior pastor coaching his team. The second level is volunteer lay cell leaders coaching the new leaders who have multiplied new cells.

***** Visit http://www.joelcomiskeygroup.com/articles/churchLeaders/statiscalReporting.htm for more information on statistical reporting.

Group coaching meetings are more necessary between the senior pastor and his team. If the senior pastor has gathered a paid staff, they should meet weekly. If the senior pastor has gathered a volunteer staff, I recommend a group meeting every fifteen days.

During those group coaching meetings, the senior pastor ministers to his key leaders through the word and prayer. Then the group talks about the cell system by carefully analyzing cell statistics, the training track, multiplication dates, and prayer needs. Like a quarterback in a huddle, the senior pastor directs the cell system through the hub of his leadership team.

I encourage volunteer leaders to continue leading a cell group while coaching up to three cell leaders. A cell coach could call each leader under his or her care once-a-month and meet with each person once a month.

In some cultures, group meetings between the volunteer coach and the cell leaders might not be as frequent. Too many "ideal" coaching structures fail because they were based on what should happen rather than what is actually happening. Thus, if time doesn't permit the volunteer coach to have a huddle meeting with cell leaders, by all means the coach should commit to the one-on-one personal time each month and a once-a-month phone call.

Some churches will have a quarterly huddle with all of the cell leaders present. The senior pastor normally leads this time.

Seventh step: plant new cell churches

Cell churches value reproduction of disciples, leaders, and cell groups. Some cell church pastors believe in multiplication at a cell level but not at a church level. Yet, it's inconsistent not to carry out multiplication at a church level as well. The logical conclusion is the reproduction of churches. Healthy churches are fruitful and multiply. The early church multiplied leaders, disciples, and churches at all levels.

The goal is to raise up a church multiplication movement. Bob Logan says, "Of all models of church, the cell church has the greatest multiplication of churches."[30]

Yet, why do some cell churches fail to multiply other churches? Often the initial vision is too small. The church planter only talks about starting one church, rather than planting multiple churches.

When Jesus saw the multitudes around Him, He said to His disciples, "Do you not say, 'Four months more and then the harvest?' I tell you, open your eyes and look at the fields! They are ripe for harvest" (John 4:35).

So often we see the multitudes but don't think about their lostness. Jesus did more than analyze their condition. He had compassion on them because ". . . they were harassed and helpless, like sheep without a shepherd" (Matthew 9:36). This compassion stirred Christ to exhort his followers to, "Ask the Lord of the harvest, therefore, to send out workers into his harvest field" (Matthew 9:36-38).

Ask God to break your heart with what breaks His heart. Then pray that the Lord of the harvest will raise up new church planters. Most likely, they'll come from among your fruitful cell leaders. Cast the vision for future church plants and be willing to hive off a group from the church to start a new work.

As you plan to start a cell church, follow the seven steps outlined above. You will make many adjustments along the way. We did in our cell church plant, and you will in yours. As Proverbs 19:21 says, "Many are the plans in a man's heart, but it is the LORD's purpose that prevails."

Chapter Nine

Planting House Churches

We've lived in Moreno Valley long enough to see myriads of houses constructed. As I've passed by the new tracks of homes, I've often dreamed of the day when those homes would be used for a dual purpose: for normal living and to reach a lost world for Jesus Christ. Traditionally, people leave their home to go to church and then go back to their homes to live. I long for the day when the church is in the home, and the planting of new churches primarily involves the use of existing homes. The early church movement flowed along those lines.

Is it possible to simply meet in homes or other facilities that can accommodate a very small number of people? This is exactly what the house church strategy proposes. And there are plenty examples of house-based churches in the New Testament.

- Church in the house of Mary (Acts 12:12).
- Church in the house of Priscilla and Aquila (Romans 16:3–5; see also 1 Corinthains 16:19).
- Church in the house of Nympha (Colossians 4:15).
- Church in the house of Archippus (Philemon v.2).

There are also examples of Jesus and early Christians going to people's homes where they would heal people, evangelize seekers, baptize entire households, and disciple new believers.[1] David Garrison says:

> House churches are stand-alone churches that happen to be small enough to meet in homes. After filling their limited space, they grow through multiplication rather than increasing their

membership. Each house church has its own leadership and derives its authority directly from Christ, rather than through a church hierarchy. It functions in every way as a church.[2]

God has time and again used the house church as a model to draw the church back to a more New Testament and simple form of church life and mission.[3]

Not only in persecuted countries

I have said repeatedly that the best application for house churches is in persecuted, resistant contexts, because persecution forced the early church to meet in homes—not because this was the preferred setting for the church. Yet, the authors of *Home Cell Groups and House Churches* make a valid point:

> It is a mistaken notion to conclude that the only reason the apostolic community developed house churches was because it was a persecuted minority and, therefore, could not go public in its institutional expression. As a matter of fact, the early church was quite public in its witness, despite the fact that it was persecuted.[4]

I still believe that the most rapid growth in the house church movement is in restricted access areas like China, Asia, and North Africa. I attended one mission gathering and heard a missionary representative for China talk about house churches springing up like wildfire. The representative spoke of one Chinese leader who had planted 30,000 churches—all house churches. This Chinese leader trains people and within three weeks they are expected to plant a church.[5]

This type of church planting doesn't take place in many contexts. There is no doubt, however, that house church ministry has become increasingly popular and accepted. Larry Kreider, co-author of *Starting a House Church*, writes:

> Within the next ten to fifteen years, I believe these new house church networks will dot the landscape of North America

just as they already do in other nations of the world. Places like China, Central Asia, Latin America, India, and Cambodia have experienced tremendous growth through house churches and disciple and empower each member to "be the church."[6]

Characteristics of house churches

My brother, Andy, has a unique personality. For starters, he has a dramatic humor that causes people to double over laughing. I don't know where he got it. In fact, often people will say, "You're kidding. Andy is your brother!" Yet Andy and I have far more in common than not. We have similar mannerisms, passions, and outlook on life. Why? DNA. Tom and Phyllis Comiskey gave birth to us and raised us under the same roof.

The house church movement has the same DNA. Yes, it's diverse. Some authors emphasize principles that others do not. Yet, common features of house churches surpass their differences. One thing is certain: house church planting offers a very simple and reproducible expression of Christ's church.

Simple structure

Ed Stetzer says, "My attraction to the house church springs from its simplicity and faith. I have been a part of large church starts. . . . Each involved more and more money. In my heart, I often feel that church planting should be simpler."[7]

The idea behind home churches is not to grow one church larger, but to keep the church intimate while reproducing other intimate fellowships in other locales.

Many New Testament church practices cannot function effectively in large, impersonal groups. Home churches form communities of believers who get to know each other in all aspects of life. They share their spiritual gifts to edify the body. Authentic Christianity has a greater chance of emerging in the lives of individuals and families because intimacy and accountability are built into the church.

The goal of each house church is to reproduce other new churches. Bob Fitts Sr. says:

> Our goal is not just to start a church. Our goal is to start a church planting movement. We believe this can best be done by focusing on the simplest and most reproducible form of church planting. The house church meets that need.[8]

One reason why house churches are reproducible is because they lack a hierarchical structure. The house church movement focuses on simple, reproducible strategies that release common Christians for uncommon work. They celebrate evangelism and reproduction that is natural and spontaneous. This reproduction is occurring at every level and in every unit of the church life. As people are released into ministry, new interdependent churches are formed.[9]

Professor Nancy T. Ammerman, sociologist of religion at Hartford Seminary, writes:

> This development [house church] shows people looking for faith's essence. They are no longer willing to finance huge buildings, a large staff, insurance policies, advertising campaigns, and the leaking church roof because it all seems simply irrelevant.[10]

One misconception of the house church movement is that all house churches meet in homes. Larry Kreider, a proponent of "house churches," started using the phrase *micro church* to highlight the fact that not all house churches meet in a house. Some will meet in coffee shops, galleries, and other places. Others prefer the term simple church, or organic church. Neil Cole, house church planter and author of *Organic Church,* plants organic churches in restaurants, bars, or other places besides homes.[11]

No clergy or "professionals" are necessary

House churches do not require ordained, seminary-trained professionals to function effectively. House churches point to the fact that New Testament teaching does not recognize clergy and laity distinctions. Those who are seminary or Bible school-trained can be assets to house churches, sometimes serving as catalysts who plant the first few house churches in a given area or people group.[12] But they don't always have to be physically present for house churches to have legitimacy or theological understanding.

One reason why house churches are reproducible is because they lack a hierarchical structure. The house church movement focuses on simple, reproducible strategies that release common Christians for uncommon work.

House churches do need godly, mature leadership (1 Timothy 3:1-12, Titus 1:5-9, 1 Peter 5:1-4). The training, however, happens primarily through an informal approach, with basic Bible knowledge and practical ministry as the main components.

Most house church leaders are volunteers. Financial resources are normally used to support itinerant workers, missions, or meeting the practical needs of members, such as the poor, widows, and orphans.

In most cases, the house church does collect an offering.[13] And in rare cases, a house church may decide to support one of the leaders. Bob Fitts Sr. writes:

A house church will be able to channel almost all of its finances into ministry. There may be some minor expenses, but since the meeting will be held in houses, all building expenses will be avoided. In this way, only ten tithing families could support a full-time pastor. Since one pastor could oversee more than one house church, he does not have to receive all his support from one congregation.[14]

No special buildings

House churches meet in ordinary homes or other places that are free from rent or payments. Maintenance and overhead related to a church building are eliminated. Larry Kreider writes:

> The Chinese house church movement has made a commitment to the Lord concerning how the church will exist even when they are freed from communism in the future. They have already made a decision that they will build no buildings. They want to keep their method of training and sending intact, and not focus on constructing buildings but on building people.[15]

The house church movement—more than any other strategy—is building-proof. Money is not spent on buildings and maintanence.

Fully the church

House churches are fully functioning churches in themselves. They partake of the Lord's supper, baptize, marry, bury, and exercise church discipline. Many house churches, however, do network with other house churches for mutual accountability, encouragement, and cooperation.

House churches are normally led by volunteers and meet for participatory meetings which involve prayer, worship, the word, and outreach. Food and fellowship are also important elements.

Simple order of meeting

There is no set order for house church meetings. One well-known house church leader suggests using five Ws (Welcome, Worship, Word, Works, and Witness) as one possibility (in appendix three I highlight four Ws as a common cell group order). Yet, most house churches have an open, participatory style with no one single order in mind.

Even when there is a more directive teaching given by the leader or one of the members, there is always plenty of time for group discussion and response to the message. The goal is to have all those present to practice their spiritual gifts. Most would agree that although certain elements may be pre-planned, there is freedom to follow the Holy Spirit, if He changes those plans.

It's common in house churches to celebrate the Lord's supper as a full meal. This often takes place at the start or end of the house church meeting, but may take place on an entirely different day. House churches point back to Acts 2:46 where the believers broke bread from house to house. Celebrating the Lord's supper as a meal can be seen in 1 Corinthians 11: 20-26, where Paul talked about participating in an actual meal.

Different Sizes

In the past, I described a house church as a community of twenty to forty people who met together on a weekly basis but were more or less independent of other house churches.

More recently, there's been a new emphasis in the house church movement. A new version of the house church promotes smaller-sized house churches. Wolfgang Simson, for example, teaches that many house churches today have between eight to fifteen members, and typically multiply every six to nine months.

Rad Zdero wrote a book called *The Global House Church Movement*. He himself planted a house church network in Canada. He writes:

House churches should not grow too large before they decide to multiply. Otherwise, the loss of intimacy, openness, and interaction will eventually compromise the group's attractiveness and plateau the numbers. Currently around the globe, explosive Christian conversion growth from church planting movement is characterized by the reproduction of multiplying house churches and cell groups of no more than 10-30 people.[16]

Starting house churches

I met a house church planting missionary in Indonesia, who told me that planting house churches was extremely simple: "The main thing is to meet friends and neighbors. Then you need to gather them in your house to hear God's word. As you make disciples of those attending, they will be prepared to start their own house churches."

Planting a house church, or movement of house churches, is all about loving people into the kingdom. The beauty is the simplicity. It's about reaching out to non-believers, gathering them in, and continuing the process with another house church. The neighbors hear the singing and worship and will ask about what's happening. An organic church doesn't depend on a building. It depends on people.

Planting a house church, or movement of house churches, is all about loving people into the kingdom.

The house church planter seeks to find people who are divinely appointed by God to hear the message and receive the gospel. He or she gathers the *persons of peace* into the small group. The goal is to meet the person's need and eventually develop him or her to be the next house church planter. Rad Zdero has adopted the motto, "Every church, start a church, every year."[17] He believes that a new house church can be planted every six to eighteen months, which seems to be the case for church planting movements in places like China and India. In my personal communications with Zdero, he cautions that this suggested timeline should not be applied mechanically; rather, the Holy Spirit must lead and open the doors for new leaders to emerge and for new house churches to start in His own time and manner (Luke 10:1-11; Acts 10:1-48, 13:1-4).

Only so many people can meet in one house. When the house church becomes too large to meet in the average-sized living room, another group is sent out to begin a house church in another place.

Whoever is called to lead the next group should be a reproducing believer who can evangelize lost people, disciple those who come to Jesus, and lead the core team in planting the next house church.

Dick Scoggins in his book, *Planting House Churches in Networks*, recommends that each house church planter writes out a clear vision of how and when to plant a new house church. From his experience in planting house churches, he warns against the dangers of *koinonitus* (inward fellowship that turns into navel gazing). Each house church planter needs to have a clear vision to reproduce.

Larry Kreider and Floyd McClung give five simple steps to staring house churches:[18]

1. Pray
2. Meet people
3. Make disciples
4. Gather
5. Multiply

It's that simple. It doesn't require a Ph.D. or years of Bible school.

One key difference between a house church and a cell church is leadership. In many house churches, the house church pastor doesn't have a higher authority but rather works cooperatively as a peer with other house church pastors. In contrast, those planting a cell in the cell church strategy are accountable to the leadership of the local church they are part of.

Networking the house churches

Many have criticized the "independence" of the house church movement—myself included. It's been refreshing to hear many house church authors making the same criticism. Many house church proponents today promote the need for house churches to network with other house churches.

Some proponents suggest gathering house churches on a monthly or quarterly basis for celebrative worship and retreats.

House church networking may also include going on mission trips with other, larger churches. The suggestion is also made by a growing number of advocates that equipping ministries of the apostles, prophets, evangelists, pastors, and teachers is not only biblical, but also absolutely essential to help launch house church networks and movements that can impact entire cities with the gospel (Acts 2:42-47, 20:17-21; Ephesians 4:11-13).[19]

Networks can function in different ways. They may be highly informal, connected only by an occasional joint gathering or special times to share ideas with one another. Or, they may be formally networked together as "sister" churches that function with common goals and projects.

Some, like Wolfgang Simson, advocate a city-church idea. According to this idea, individual house churches (although full-fledged churches in themselves) also seek out broader fellowship with other house churches and/or traditional churches in the city. A particular house church might collaborate with the First Christian Church or Central Assembly of God to engage in cross-congregational ministry. Some in the house church movement believe that the city-wide church concept is one of the most important expressions of the local church. They base this on the fact that the New Testament writers refer to a single "church" (Greek = *ekklēsia*) of this or that city (Romans 16:1; 1 Corinthians 1:2, etc.). Bill Beckham has analyzed this view in detail (see this endnote for more detail).[20]

No matter how house churches network, a growing consensus insists that house churches must avoid an exclusive and ingrown mentality.[21] Rad Zdero writes:

> It is absolutely crucial that house churches form networks that pray, plan, and play together. So long as house churches choose isolation, independence, and inwardness, so long will they remain a mere novelty, a trend, a fad, without ever becoming a real movement that deeply impacts their city, region, or nation with the gospel of Christ. They must unite![22]

Cell churches and house church networks are cousins

House church networks and cell churches have much more in common than not. Both find their basis for ministry in the New Testament—not just in a general way but in a specific one. Both see clear references to cell-celebration and to house churches. Both long for simplicity—less programs and professionalism and more emphasis on developing disciples who make disciples.

I believe, in fact, that Jesus is calling His church back to a New Testament emphasis. House church networks and cell churches are leading the way. Larry Kreider, an advocate of both cell churches and house church networks, writes:

> DOVE Christian Fellowship International, the worldwide network of cell-based churches that I and a team of spiritual leaders oversee, is broadening our territory to include house church networks. We realize that cell-based community churches, cell-based mega-churches and house church networks, although different, are close cousins. Our experience thus far has been mostly with cells in a mega-church and with cells in community churches.[23]

I've talked with Larry Kreider on various occasions about the differences between cell churches and house church networks. During a recent conversation I asked him about the new micro churches that Dove is establishing. He gave an example of one of the Dove house church networks where he actually attends. Each of the house churches in the network meets weekly, but then the network of house churches come together approximately once a month to celebrate. Kreider thinks that the most healthy house churches meet together on a regular basis (normally once per month).

"But this is exactly what we're doing at Wellspring, the church I planted," I told him. The life groups meet weekly and come together to celebrate once a month. Granted, we are actively looking for a place to hold weekly celebrations. Yet, some cell churches will never choose to meet weekly in celebration. So what's the key difference?

Larry mentioned that one difference was the way house churches keep the offering. In the house church network that he is coaching, the house churches give a percentage of the money to the network so that both individual house churches and the network determine how the money will be spent.

"I don't see much difference here," I told him. "I've observed cell churches that pool their money in a similar way. The cells and the cell networks decide how the money will be spent. Often the individual cells will use the money on outreach and other projects."

Both Larry and I agreed that house church networks are more informal and give more liberty to each house church. Yet, it seems to be a matter of degree. Cell church networks can also be flexible. We also agreed that whether or not someone uses the terminology *cell church* or *house church network*, the important thing is that the Great Commission is being fulfilled.

I shared with Larry my concerns that house church leaders were not receiving enough coaching. Kreider admitted that coaching is essential. He felt that house church networks need help to assure that each house church leader is properly coached.

I asked him what he did with children in his house church. He told me that often the children in the micro church will meet with the adults in the beginning but will then go into another room for their own Bible time.

"This is exactly what we do in many of our life groups," I told him.

My bias: cell church or connected house church

Simple house church planting and cell church planting share much in common. I do believe, however, that a cell church or house church network should highlight certain characteristics.

House church leaders need coaching

I believe that leaders need coaching. Yes, the Holy Spirit is the great coach, but He uses humans to get the job done.

Isolated house church leaders or cell leaders are not nearly as effective as those who have a coach.

Michael Jordan needed a coach. Why would Michael Jordan need a coach? Because the coach could help Jordan maximize his game, take a rest when needed, defend against over-zealous players, and point out the overlooked details of the game. Players look at the immediate task, but the coach is able to provide the bigger picture.

Small group leaders left to themselves (whether cell leader or house church leaders) become less effective. My journey in the cell church world has taught me that coaching is a critical component.

In the cell church scheme (or the connected house church paradigm), the coach plays a crucial role. In fact, each leader has a coach to assure fruitfulness and to help the leader achieve the God-given goals.

In the cell church scheme (or the connected house church paradigm) the coach plays an intimate role to assure fruitfulness. Another important reason for coaching is to achieve rapid multiplication. It's more difficult to develop an independent leader than a networked one who has a coach. I think it would be difficult to raise up an independent pastor of a group of six to twelve people. It's far more likely that the person will step up to the plate, if he or she knows that coaching will occur on a regular basis. Kreider says:

> The house church and cell group provide an ideal opportunity for everyone to experience a spiritual family and eventually become spiritual parents themselves. The purpose for house church multiplication and cell multiplication is to give the opportunity for new parents to take responsibility to start a new spiritual family (house church and cell groups).[24]

Need for a shared equipping track

A small group leader (cell leader or house church leader) should not have to decide what training he or she should receive. Cell churches or house church networks should lay out a training path to maintain quality. In my book, *Leadership Explosion*, I share principles that cell churches use to train their leaders to multiply groups. A church can greatly increase their effectiveness by providing clear-cut training, rather than hoping that an independent leader will find his or her way. For example, Xenos Christian Fellowship has networked their house churches into an organized structure to assure the quality training (see appendix six).

Strength in groups coming together to celebrate

As mentioned earlier, a house church or cell network does not have to meet weekly; however, they should meet regularly for both teaching and encouragement. In restricted access countries, it's not possible to hold a celebration service. In free countries, however, where this is possible, the church should take advantage of the opportunity to gather for a celebration service.

A spirit of independence is always dangerous and should be avoided like the plague. Bill Beckham says, "I believe the New Testament design of the church will express itself someway at the local level in both large-group and small-group life." [25] I think that the large group gatherings should be planned to make sure they actually happen. It seems idealistic to simply "hope" they will happen. Why not plan for the cells/house churches to come together on a regular basis? The celebration refreshes the leaders, provides impetus for outreach, and glorifies God as His people worship in unity.

Planting churches that reproduce requires simplicity, but they must not be left alone. Leaders need coaching, training, and the refreshment of meeting together to worship God and press on. And the goal is not to plant just one church but a movement of churches—a church planting movement. David Garrison writes:

> It is important to understand the role of small house and cell churches in the life of a Church Planting Movement. It's now easy to see why missionaries who want to start a Church Planting Movement without house or cell churches will find it so difficult. [26]

God is using cell churches and house church networks to reproduce church planting movements all over the world.

Chapter Ten

Simple Reproduction

I often tell leaders to guide the group in such a way that anyone could say, "I can do what John is doing." Or "I could lead like Nancy." I visited one group in which the leader rattled off numerous Greek words. *Is she trying to impress me with her knowledge?* I thought to myself. She liberally quoted Bible commentators and ended up teaching ninety percent of the lesson. When others dared to comment, she hesitantly acknowledged them. Quickly, however, she cut them off, preferring her own authoritative voice. When I left the group, I realized that few people would volunteer to lead the next group. The leader set herself up as a Bible authority. The group lacked simplicity and reproducibility.

Simple reproduction characterizes effective church plants. Churches that plant churches possess a DNA for planting new churches that is simple enough to follow. Charles Brock, a missionary church planter, wrote:

> If the church is to reproduce itself, the planter must use a church planting strategy . . . on the people's level of understanding. Simplicity has a beauty appreciated by all who are searching for God. The strategy should be within the mental grasp of anyone who desires to plant a new church.[1]

Simplicity

God uses ordinary people to do extraordinary work. Jesus modeled this principle by choosing the common people of His day to become His followers. None of Christ's disciples occupied important positions in the synagogue, nor did any of them belong to the Levitical priesthood. Rather, they were common laboring men, having no professional training, no academic degrees, and no source of inherited wealth. Most were raised in the poor part of the country. They were impulsive, temperamental, and easily offended. Jesus broke through the barriers that separated the clean and unclean, the obedient and sinful.

He summoned fisherman as well as a tax collector and zealot. Jesus saw hidden potential in them. He detected a teachable spirit, honesty, and a willingness to learn. They possessed a hunger for God, a sincerity to look beyond the religious hypocrisy of their day, and in turn, they were looking for someone to lead them to salvation.

Likewise, spontaneous church planting is taking place all over the world as ordinary believers step up to plant churches. Just like the early church equipped and released people to minister, we need to set people free to serve. David Garrison writes:

> When discipleship and leadership development are contained in the DNA of the first churches, they will naturally transfer that DNA to their offspring. The opposite is also true. When you teach your first churches to labor for many years under a missionary pastor while waiting to receive their own seminary trained leader. . . you can't expect them to generate rapidly reproducing daughter churches. Rapid reproduction starts with the DNA of the first church.[2]

Education is important; a person should obtain as much as possible. I've noticed, however, that the exciting church planting movements taking place around the world don't depend on seminary training to produce new church planters. They look to fruitful leaders within the church itself, who are willing to pastor the new churches. Many churches have their own Bible training within the church or a clear-cut way to prepare future church planters. Some of them have reached a place of spontaneous expansion—a movement that has a life of its own.

Roland Allen wrote *The Spontaneous Expansion of the Church and Causes Which Hinder It* in 1927. Allen's book is as relevant today as when he wrote it eighty years ago. He writes:

By spontaneous expansion I mean something which we cannot control. And if we cannot control it, we ought, as I think, to rejoice that we cannot control it. For if we cannot control it, it is because it is too great not because it is too small for us. The great things of God are beyond our control. Therein lies a vast hope.[3]

God is taking His church to a place of spontaneous multiplication, like a flowing river that makes its own path. When church planting is simple and reproducible, many will get involved, and expansion will occur.

Humans can't easily categorize God's multiplication movements because they are spontaneous and even messy. (One professor of Christian movements said to me, "Revival is always messy.") Even though God's work flows by its own current, we can participate in it. And God wants us to jump into the stream and allow Him to use us. One of the core principles of God's growing movements around the world is reproduction.

Reproduction

God loves reproduction; it's at the core of His creation. God's desire for reproduction is seen in the first chapter of Genesis: "God blessed mankind saying, 'Be fruitful and increase in number; fill the earth and subdue it. Rule over the fish of the sea and the birds of the air and over every living creature that moves on the ground'" (Genesis 1:28).

Stuart Murray, citing Genesis chapter one as pointing to the Spirit's original and unchanging desire to engender fruitfulness and multiplication, writes, "The parenting of new congregations. . . is a natural instinct of those born again by this Spirit and gathered by him into local Christian families."[4]

In a similar fashion, God blessed Abraham at the age of ninety-nine saying, "I will confirm my covenant between me and you and will greatly increase your numbers" (Genesis 17:2). Jesus commands the same type of fruitfulness in John 15:8: "This is to my Father's glory, that you bear much fruit, showing yourselves to be my disciples." At the end of His ministry, Jesus said to His disciples: "All authority in heaven and on earth has been given to me. Therefore go and make disciples of all nations, baptizing them in the name of the Father and of the Son and of the Holy Spirit" (Matthew 28:18-19). The only viable way to reap the harvest is through planting new churches.

Our natural, human tendency steers us toward the norm. We want the warmth and communion of the church plant to continue forever. It won't. In refreshing others, we are refreshed. Church members will grow stronger when they lead others. Some will even plant new churches.

Reproduction is the core theme of church planting. Effective church plants tailor their vision and training to fulfill the objective of planting new churches. The genetic code of church planting is instilled in the church from the moment it begins.

Robert J. Vajko did his doctoral study on why churches reproduce other churches. He discovered that one key factor was a vision, from the beginning, to reproduce. Churches that planted churches had a vision to plant new churches from the start.[5] Planting new churches is so central that it deserves the first place in the church's focus. The primary goal is to plant a new one.

God's on your side

The good news is that God stands behind church planters. He wants them to prosper and bear fruit—more than they want it to happen. Our job is to hang in there long enough for God to come through. In his book, *From Good to Great*, Jim Collins compares companies that have exceeded expectations over a long period of time with companies that met some expectations but didn't excel. One of the key reasons for the growth of the successful companies was what Collins labels "the flywheel." He says:

> In building greatness, there is no single defining action, no grand program, no one killer innovation, no solitary lucky break, no miracle moment. Rather, the process resembles relentlessly pushing a giant, heavy flywheel in one direction, turn upon turn, building momentum until a point of breakthrough and beyond.[6]

The great companies kept turning the flywheel—even in difficult times—and eventually, from imparted momentum, the flywheel began to turn on its own.

Disappointments and trials part of the job description of a church planter. One reason many church plants fail, however, is because the church planter gives up too early. They don't keep "turning the flywheel" until the breakthrough occurs. Tim, a church planter I'm coaching from Texas, has been doing all the right things since he started the church three years ago, but he still has not seen the results he desires. I told Tim to keep turning the flywheel. "Keep pressing on. God will give you the breakthrough, and there will be a harvest of people in His time. Remember that He is more interested in saving the lost and making disciples than you are."

Paul's words in Romans can be applied directly to church planters, "What, then, shall we say in response to this? If God is for us, who can be against us? He who did not spare his own Son, but gave him up for us all—how will he not also, along with him, graciously give us all things?" (Romans 8:31–32).

Resources by Joel Comiskey

Joel Comiskey's previous books cover the following topics

- Leading a cell group (*How to Lead a Great Cell Group Meeting, 2001*).
- How to multiply the cell group (*Home Cell Group Explosion, 1998*).
- How to prepare spiritually for cell ministry (*An Appointment with the King, 2002*).
- How to practically organize your cell system (*Reap the Harvest,1999; Cell Church Explosion, 2004*).
- How to train future cell leaders (*Leadership Explosion, 2001; Live, 2007; Encounter, 2007; Grow, 2007; Share, 2007; Lead, 2007; Coach, 2008; Discover, 2008*).
- How to coach/care for cell leaders (*How to be a Great Cell Group Coach, 2003; Groups of Twelve, 2000; From Twelve to Three, 2002*).
- How the gifts of the Spirit work within the cell group (*The Spirit-filled Small Group, 2005*).
- How to fine tune your cell system (*Making Cell Groups Work Navigation Guide, 2003*).
- Principles from the second largest church in the world (*Passion and Persistence, 2004*).
- How cell church works in North America (*The Church that Multiplies, 2007*).

All of the books listed are available from Joel Comiskey Group by calling toll-free **1-888-344-CELL**(2355) or by ordering online at:
www.joelcomiskeygroup.com

How To Lead A Great Cell Group Meeting: So People Want to Come Back

Do people expectantly return to your group meetings every week? Do you have fun and experience joy during your meetings? Is everyone participating in discussion and ministry? You can lead a great cell group meeting, one that is life changing and dynamic. Most people don't realize that they can create a God-filled atmosphere because they don't know how. Now the secret is out. This guide will show you how to:

- Prepare yourself spiritually to hear God during the meeting
- Structure the meeting so it flows
- Spur people in the group to participate and share their lives openly
- Share your life with others in the group
- Create stimulating questions
- Listen effectively to discover what is transpiring in others' lives
- Encourage and edify group members
- Open the group to non-Christians
- See the details that create a warm atmosphere

By implementing these time-tested ideas, your group meetings will become the hot-item of your members' week. They will go home wanting more and return each week bringing new people with them. 140 pgs.

Home Cell Group Explosion: How Your Small Group Can Grow and Multiply

The book crystallizes the author's findings in some eighteen areas of research, based on a meticulous questionnaire that he submitted to cell church leaders in eight countries around the world, locations that he also visited personally for his research. The detailed notes in the back of the book offer the student of cell church growth a rich mine for further reading. The beauty of Comiskey's book is that he not only summarizes his survey results in a thoroughly convincing way but goes on to analyze in practical ways many of his survey results in separate chapters. The happy result is that any cell church leader, intern or member completing this quick read will have his priorities/values clearly aligned and ready to be followed-up. If you are a pastor or small group leader, you should devour this book! It will encourage you and give you simple, practical steps for dynamic small group life and growth. 175 pgs.

An Appointment with the King: *Ideas for Jump-Starting Your Devotional Life*

With full calendars and long lists of things to do, people often put on hold life's most important goal: building an intimate relationship with God. Often, believers wish to pursue the goal but are not sure how to do it. They feel frustrated or guilty when their attempts at personal devotions seem empty and unfruitful. With warm, encouraging writing, Joel Comiskey guides readers on how to set a daily appointment with the King and make it an exciting time they will look forward to. This book first answers the question "Where do I start?" with step-by-step instructions on how to spend time with God and practical ideas for experiencing him more fully. Second, it highlights the benefits of spending time with God, including joy, victory over sin, and spiritual guidance. The book will help Christians tap into God's resources on a daily basis, so that even in the midst of busyness they can walk with him in intimacy and abundance. 175 pgs.

Reap the Harvest: *How a Small Group System Can Grow Your Church*

Have you tried small groups and hit a brick wall? Have you wondered why your groups are not producing the fruit that was promised? Are you looking to make your small groups more effective? Cell-church specialist and pastor Dr. Joel Comiskey studied the world's most successful cell churches to determine why they grow. The key: They have embraced specific principles. Conversely, churches that do not embrace these same principles have problems with their groups and therefore do not grow. Cell churches are successful not because they have small groups but because they can support the groups. In this book, you will discover how these systems work. 236 pgs.

La Explosión de la Iglesia Celular: *Cómo Estructurar la Iglesia en Células Eficaces* (Editorial Clie, 2004)

This book is only available in Spanish and contains Joel Comiskey's research of eight of the world's largest cell churches, five of which reside in Latin America. It details how to make the transition from a traditional church to the cell church structure and many other valuable insights, including: the history of the cell church, how to organize your church to become a praying church, the most important principles of the cell church, and how to raise up an army of cell leaders. 236 pgs.

Leadership Explosion: *Multiplying Cell Group Leaders to Reap the Harvest*

Some have said that cell groups are leader breeders. Yet even the best cell groups often have a leadership shortage. This shortage impedes growth and much of the harvest goes untouched. Joel Comiskey has discovered why some churches are better at raising up new cell leaders than others. These churches do more than pray and hope for new leaders. They have an intentional strategy, a plan that will quickly equip as many new leaders as possible. In this book, you will discover the training models these churches use to multiply leaders. You will discover the underlying principles of these models so that you can apply them.
202 pgs.

FIVE-BOOK EQUIPPING SERIES

| #1: Live | #2: Encounter | #3: Grow | #4: Share | #5: Lead |

The five book equipping series is designed to train a new believer all the way to leading his or her own cell group. Each of the five books contains eight lessons. Each lesson has interactive activities that helps the trainee reflect on the lesson in a personal, practical way.

Live starts the training by covering key Christian doctrines, including baptism and the Lord's supper. 85 pgs.

Encounter guides the believer to receive freedom from sinful bondages. The Encounter book can be used one-on-one or in a group. 91 pgs.

Grow gives step-by-step instruction for having a daily quiet time, so that the believer will be able to feed him or herself through spending daily time with God. 87 pgs.

Share instructs the believer how to communicate the gospel message in a winsome, personal way. This book also has two chapters on small group evangelism. 91 pgs.

Lead prepares the Christian on how to facilitate an effective cell group. This book would be great for those who form part of a small group team. 91 pgs.

TWO-BOOK ADVANCED TRAINING SERIES

COACH   **DISCOVER**

Coach and Discover make-up the Advanced Training, prepared specifically to take a believer to the next level of maturity in Christ.

Coach prepares a believer to coach another cell leader. Those experienced in cell ministry often lack understanding on how to coach someone else. This book provides step-by-step instruction on how to coach a new cell leader from the first meeting all the way to giving birth to a new group. The book is divided into eight lessons, which are interactive and help the potential coach deal with real-life, practical coaching issues. 85 pgs.

Discover clarifies the twenty gifts of the Spirit mentioned in the New Testament. The second part shows the believer how to find and use his or her particular gift. This book is excellent to equip cell leaders to discover the giftedness of each member in the group. 91 pgs.

  ***How to be a Great Cell Group Coach:*** *Practical insight for Supporting and Mentoring Cell Group Leaders*

Research has proven that the greatest contributor to cell group success is the quality of coaching provided for cell group leaders. Many are serving in the position of a coach, but they don't fully understand what they are supposed to do in this position. Joel Comiskey has identified seven habits of great cell group coaches. These include: Receiving from God, Listening to the needs of the cell group leader, Encouraging the cell group leader, Caring for the multiple aspects of a leader's life, Developing the cell leader in various aspects of leadership, Strategizing with the cell leader to create a plan, Challenging the cell leader to grow.

Practical insights on how to develop these seven habits are outlined in section one. Section two addresses how to polish your skills as a coach with instructions on diagnosing problems in a cell group, how to lead coaching meetings, and what to do when visiting a cell group meeting. This book will prepare you to be a great cell group coach, one who mentors, supports, and guides cell group leaders into great ministry. 139 pgs.

Groups of Twelve: *A New Way to Mobilize Leaders and Multiply Groups in Your Church*

This book clears the confusion about the Groups of 12 model. Joel dug deeply into the International Charismatic Mission in Bogota, Colombia and other G12 churches to learn the simple principles that G12 has to offer your church. This book also contrasts the G12 model with the classic 5x5 and shows you what to do with this new model of ministry. Through onsite research, international case studies, and practical experience, Joel Comiskey outlines the G12 principles that your church can use today.

Billy Hornsby, director of the Association of Related Churches, says, "Joel Comiskey shares insights as a leader who has himself raised up numerous leaders. From how to recognize potential leaders to cell leader training to time-tested principles of leadership--this book has it all. The accurate comparisons of various training models make it a great resource for those who desire more leaders. Great book!" 182 pgs.

From Twelve To Three: *How to Apply G12 Principles in Your Church*

The concept of the Groups of 12 began in Bogota, Colombia, but now it is sweeping the globe. Joel Comiskey has spent years researching the G12 structure and the principles behind it.

From his experience as a pastor, trainer, and consultant, he has discovered that there are two ways to embrace the G12 concept: adopting the entire model or applying the principles that support the model.

This book focuses on the application of principles rather than adoption of the entire model. It outlines the principles and provides a modified application which Joel calls the G12.3. This approach presents a pattern that is adaptable to many different church contexts.

The concluding section illustrates how to implement the G12.3 in various kinds of churches, including church plants, small churches, large churches, and churches that already have cells. 178 pgs.

The Spirit-filled Small Group: *Leading Your Group to Experience the Spiritual Gifts.*
The focus in many of today's small groups has shifted from Spirit-led transformation to just another teacher-student Bible study. But exercising every member's spiritual gifts is vital to the effectiveness of the group. With insight born of experience in more than twenty years of small group ministry, Joel Comiskey explains how leaders and participants alike can be supernaturally equipped to deal with real-life issues. Put these principles into practice and your small group will never be the same!

This book works well with Comiskey's training book, ***Discover.*** It fleshes out many of the principles in Comiskey's training book. Chuck Crismier, radio host, Viewpoint, writes, "Joel Comiskey has again provided the Body of Christ with an important tool to see God's Kingdom revealed in and through small groups." 191 pgs.

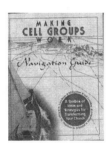

Making Cell Groups Work Navigation Guide: *A Toolbox of Ideas and Strategies for Transforming Your Church.*
For the first time, experts in cell group ministry have come together to provide you with a 600 page reference tool like no other. When Ralph Neighbour, Bill Beckham, Joel Comiskey and Randall Neighbour compiled new articles and information under careful orchestration and in-depth understanding that Scott Boren brings to the table, it's as powerful as private consulting! Joel Comiskey has an entire book within this mammoth 600 page work. There are also four additional authors.

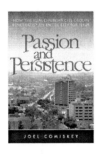 

Passion and Persistence: *How the Elim Church's Cell Groups Penetrated an Entire City for Jesus*

This book describes how the Elim Church in San Salvador grew from a small group to 116,000 people in 10,000 cell groups. Comiskey takes the principles from Elim and applies them to churches in North America and all over the world.

Ralph Neighbour says: "I believe this book will be remember as one of the most important ever written about a cell church movement! I experienced the *passion* when visiting Elim many years ago. Comiskey's report about Elim is not a *pattern* to be slavishly copied. It is a journey into grasping the true theology and methodology of the New Testament church. You'll discover how the Elim Church fans into flame their passion for Jesus and His Word, how they organize their cells to penetrate a city and world for Jesus, and how they persist until God brings the fruit." 158 pgs.

The Church that Multiplies: *Growing a Healthy Cell Church in North America.*

Does the cell church strategy work in North America? We hear about exciting cell churches in Colombia and Korea, but where are the dynamic North American cell churches? This book not only declares that the cell church concept does work in North America but dedicates an entire chapter to examining North American churches that are successfully using the cell strategy to grow in quality and quantity. This book provides the latest statistical research about the North American church and explains why the cell church approach restores health and growth to the church today. More than anything else, this book will provide practical solutions for pastors and lay leaders to use in implementing cell-based ministry. 181 pgs.

Additional Options

Church plants come in many forms. The Evangelical Free website says:

> Some specialists claim there are as many as 30 methods. These range from a parent church "hiving" off a large group of members to a planter arriving in a town and knocking on doors. The exact method used will depend on many factors, and should be chosen only after careful consideration of the planters gifts, theology, philosophy of ministry, and more. The planter should seek much wise counsel and prayer support[1]

Elmer Towns lists six ways to plant a church

1. Mother-daughter church planting
2. Mission Sunday school
3. Bible study group, which senses a growing burden to organize into a church
4. Local association church planting
5. Church splits
6. Pioneer church planting[2]

Peter Wagner notes twelve ways to plant a church

Modality models (from church structures)

1. Hiving off daughter
2. Colonization (daughter is hived off in another geographical area)
3. Adoption (someone else plants the church but your church adopts them)

4. Accidental parenthood (a split of some kind)
5. The satellite model (not complete autonomy for the new congregation)
6. Multi-congregational churches (various ethnic churches using the same facility)
7. Multiple campus model (various churches meet in same facilities but different parts of that facility)

Sodality models (from mission structures)

1. The mission team
2. The catalytic church planter
3. The founding pastor
4. The independent church planter
5. The apostolic church planter[3]

Who Initiates the church plant?

Congregation Initiated

History indicates that many churches that start new churches experience their own revitalization and both congregations reap the benefits of such endeavors. It is important to note that the new congregation needs to be empowered to make its own decisions from an early point in the process of development.

Individual Initiated

When an individual conceives a vision for a new church start, that person can work with their region and the new church ministry team to assess feasibility and discern the planter's calling to this work. Should all participants be in agreement, the individual assembles resources and works toward implementing their vision. In the first three years of the new church movement, the majority of our new congregations have started using this model. Aquila and Priscilla planted their own church (1 Corinthians 16:19; Romans 16:3-5).

Region Initiated

In some cases a region will identify a good target location and do the initial work towards developing a ministry plan and gathering a core group for a new church project. The region will also perform a search for a church planter and facilitate the early stages of development. In rare cases, the New Church Ministry Team has taken this role itself, but generally they partner with the sponsoring Region.

Affiliations

There are existing congregations that are not affiliated with any denomination that seek to be in relationship with a particular movement or denomination. In some cases these congregations have existed for a long time. However, the majority of these communities are newly formed. Many ethnic congregations fit this model since the organized denominations of their home country do not exist in the US or Canada.

Splits

Occasionally, an existing church decides to split or a group chooses to leave the church. In such cases, the Region must always be involved if a new church is to emerge.

Order for the First Cell

When starting a pilot small group, whether a cell or organic church, I recommend the four Ws. While I don't believe there is only one agenda, the following one, described below, works well. The four Ws offer maximum participation of group members and is easy to follow.*

The four Ws

Each of the four Ws has a specific purpose. The icebreaker (welcome) helps people to experience the group dynamic. Prayer and singing (worship) directs people's attention to the living God. The Bible time (word) applies God's word to daily living. Finally, the members are encouraged to share the good news with others (witness).

Welcome (15 minutes)

The welcome normally includes some kind of icebreaker: What do you like to do on vacation? What is your favorite hobby? The idea is to connect each person in the group to everyone else. The welcome time lasts about 15 minutes.

---

* My book How to Lead a Great Cell Group Meeting goes into much more detail about how to lead a cell group. For more information, go to www.joelcomiskeygroup.com.

Worship (20 minutes)

The worship time centers on God, who He is and what He has done. The cell exists to give glory to God, and the worship time initiates that process. Whether you have an instrument or not, the goal is to give Him glory through worship. You can worship through singing songs, praying, reading a Psalm, or meditating on God in silence. Provide a song sheet with the songs listed for that evening (normally 4-5 songs on the sheet). Don't worry if no one is present to play a guitar or piano. You can always use a worship CD or worship without accompanying music. In between the songs, the worship leader should allow group members to offer a sentence praise, prayer, or silent confession.

Word (40 minutes)

The word time allows God to speak directly to His people through the Scriptures. Great leaders draw out others to share their thoughts and apply God's word. Cell lessons normally have about three to seven questions based on God's word.

The best cell leaders are facilitators—not Bible teachers or preachers. Cell leaders should not talk too much because the goal is not information, but *transformation*. Great leaders help steer the group away from talking about world politics, criticism of the church, or the opinions of different authors. Again, the goal is to apply God's word to daily living. People should go away changed by God's eternal message.

To begin, ask members to read the Bible verses out loud. However, only ask people to read who you know are confident readers in public. Some like to have the verses printed on a sheet of paper beforehand, using a reader-friendly translation, so everyone can follow along.

Then give a brief explanation of the Bible passage. Make sure to not preach; however, members won't know how to answer the questions unless they grasp the meaning of the passage. The leader should take about ten minutes to explain the main points of the Bible passage. A leader doesn't need to be a Bible expert to do this.

Many churches base their cell lessons on the Sunday morning preaching, and thus, cell leaders can take notes while the pastor is preaching the message, knowing that he or she will be covering that topic during the cell meeting the following week. If the cell lesson is not connected with the sermon, the leader will prepare by reviewing the Bible verses before the cell meeting.

Witness (15 minutes)

The witness time is the last part of the cell group. It focuses on reaching out to others, which may be planning an evangelistic activity, planning some kind of practical social action ministry, or simply praying in the group for friends and family who need Jesus.

To give you an idea of what a cell lesson might look like, a sample cell lesson that I've used on a number of occasions, is provided below. This sample will give you an idea of the four parts of the cell and how each part flows together.

My own life group

Let me give you an example of the cell that meets in my home every Sunday night. We start with an icebreaker (welcome). "If someone were to ask you a question that's guaranteed to get you talking, what would that question be?" The purpose is to figuratively break the ice—to ease people into fellowship with one another. We always welcome newcomers and non-Christians.

Then we seek the Lord through a time of singing and prayer (worship). Each person receives a song sheet. Sometimes I pick the songs, while at times others choose. Flexibility reigns. What's important is that we enter into the presence of Jesus Christ.

Next, we enter the cell lesson (word). The cell lesson is lively and full of participation. My role is facilitator—not Bible teacher. I'm successful when each member has applied the biblical passage to their own lives. During the cell lesson, through the Holy Spirit, God applies his Word to the specific needs of those present. After the lesson, I ask for specific prayer requests. We pray one for another. Often we'll lay hands on someone who is hurting.

Last, I share the vision for outreach (witness). I might say: "Who will you invite next week?" or "Let's remember to pray for Bob, who will lead the next daughter cell group."

Our cell meeting (no longer than 1 ½ hours) closes with a refreshment time. Some stay for an additional hour, while others leave. Some of the best ministry times occur after the cell group in the afterglow of God's presence.

Cells are flexible yet consistent. No two cells are exactly alike, but each cell maintains the same components: seeking God (worship, prayer, and lesson), developing relationships with one another (ice-breaker, ministry to one another, and refreshment time), and reaching out to non-Christians (friendship evangelism, special cell activity, and multiplication).

Sample cell meeting

Welcome: icebreaker questions

- Where did you live between the ages of seven to twelve?
- How many brothers and sisters did you have?
- Who was the person you felt closest to?
- What is your favorite sport?

Worship

- Read Psalm 8 aloud in unison.
- Sing "Amazing Grace."
- Read Psalm 29; let each person read a verse in turn.
- Ask for a period of silence for one minute; encourage the members to consider the ways God has comforted them in past situations.

Word

- Read 2 Corinthians 1:3–5.
- Ask, "Share a time when you were in a crisis and God comforted you."
- After a time of sharing, then ask, "Can you recall a time when you were used by God to comfort someone else?"
- Finally, ask, "Who in our group is in need of God's comfort right now?"
- Edify one another as God opens the way to comfort one another.

Witness

- Share names and circumstances of unbelievers who are going through difficult times.
- Discuss how we as a cell might witness to these unbelievers by becoming God's agents of comfort in their time of distress.

Cell Church Principles

I have listed below the common patterns or principles that I observed in the eight largest worldwide cell churches. If you'd like more in-depth information, please read my book *Reap the Harvest*, Chapter 3, "Principles for Building a Strong Cell System." The first four principles are the most important, in my opinion.

1. Dependence on Jesus Christ through prayer.

2. Senior pastor and leadership team giving strong, visionary leadership to the cell ministry.

3. Cell ministry promoted as the backbone of the church.

4. Clear definition of a cell group (weekly, outside the church building, evangelistic, pastoral care and discipleship, clear goal of multiplication).

5. The passion behind cell ministry is evangelism and church growth.

6. Reproduction (multiplication) is the major goal of each cell group.

7. Cell and celebration attendance expected of everyone attending the church.

8. Clearly established leadership requirements for those entering cell ministry.

9. Required cell leadership training for all potential cell group leaders.

10. Cell leadership developed from within the church itself, at all levels.

11. A supervisory care structure for each level of leadership (G-12 or 5x5).

12. Follow-up system of visitors and new converts administered through cell groups.

13. Cell lessons based on pastor's teaching to promote continuity between cell and celebration (although flexibility might be given to meet the needs of specific homogeneous groups).

Bill Beckham and Celebration

Bill Beckham found various levels of evidence for the large group wing of the church.[1]

Evidence from Scripture

- Acts 1 The whole church waits in one accord to receive God's promise
- Acts 2 The whole church in evangelism and witness
- Acts 3 The whole church preaching after a healing
- Acts 5 The whole church in great fear because of Ananias and Sapphira
- Acts 7 The whole church ministering to the needs of the church
- Acts 7 The whole church solving a problem
- Acts 7 The whole church chooses the Seven
- Acts 11 Peter explains about the conversion of Gentiles
- Acts 11 Barnabas and Saul teach the church at Antioch
- Acts 12 The whole church in prayer for Peter in prison
- Acts 13 The whole church at Antioch selects Barnabas and Saul
- Acts 14 The whole Antioch church hears the first missionary report

Evidence from the Nature of New Testament Meetings

The Church at Pentecost expressed itself in several different types and sizes of meetings without special buildings. They met (possibly all within the course of one day) in the Upper Room as a "congregation" local expression, in the Temple courtyard as a "universal" public expression and in the homes of Christians as a small group expression. And Paul spoke to gatherings of many different types and sizes without the benefit of a special church building. However, the absence of church buildings did not hinder the early expansion of the Church because the church did meet in informal large groups along with the small groups. Another practical factor sheds further light upon the early church and it's meeting places.

Benches, chairs, and pews were not used in the early centuries. Therefore, much larger groups could assemble in smaller rooms. Hence, 120 were in the upper room of a house in Jerusalem on the day of Pentecost.

Evidence from Persecution

Most "House Churches" in areas of persecution such as China find a way to function in both a large group and small group expression. In times of persecution the church raises the public large group expression just as high as it will go before the government chops it off. The church then operates in a large group expression up to that level of persecution until the government relaxes or increases the pressure.

Evidence from New Testament Leadership

Leadership in the New Testament operates beyond a strictly small group or house church level. In Paul's system the leader roles of Elder and Deacon functioned beyond the single cell "house church" level. The mix of Bishops, Elders, and Deacons implies that the church also operated in a larger local body configuration. A balanced two-wing approach gives a way for these different types of New Testament leaders to work in a New Testament way.

The Absence of a Large Group

The house church expression has periodically surfaced in church history for two reasons. One, when outside political powers has prohibited a large group expression, the church has been forced into a small group expression. The church in China today is an example of this. Two, from time to time radical or revival elements in the church have reacted to large group abuses or weaknesses and have reshaped the church into a small group configuration.

Xenos Christian Fellowship

Xenos Christian Fellowship in Ohio views itself as a group of house churches that network together for teaching and worship.

At one time the church was made up of independent house churches that were more generally linked together. However, the church decided to start exercising more control of the house churches and hold celebrations each week. When this happened about half of the house churches left because they wanted their independence.

Xenos sees itself as an underground indigenous house church planting movement. Underground means that their growth is primarily through neighborhood groups, not through large worship services or seekers meetings. It also implies the leaders of home churches are all lay people (i.e. they are not professionals, but "tentmakers"). Even when staffers lead home groups, they receive no compensation for that part of their ministry.

Indigenous, means the leadership for the home churches has to come from within the home churches themselves via a process of personal discipleship. Xenos also fields a large central leadership and programs directed by paid staff. The reason they do so is because:

- The early church seems to have had unified elderships in each city, but multiple house churches. For instance, the church in Jerusalem had thousands attending, but they all related to the single eldership of the apostles, while also meeting "from house to house." (Compare Acts 2:41; 42; 46).
- In Ephesus, the group must have numbered in the hundreds or (more likely) the thousands, judging from the size of the pile of books and charms they burned (Acts 19:19), yet they had a single eldership (Acts 20:17). These examples suggest the existence of

both self-replicating house churches and a central leadership group.

- Xenos also sees the early church's ability to form special ministry teams or programs, like collections for the poor in Judea or mission teams to go out to other cities (Acts 11:28-30, 13:1-3, 2 Cor. 8:9). Specialized teams or programs are appropriate for specialized ministries.

Xenos thinks house churches can draw strength from each other by banding together for these special cooperative, joint ministry projects and programs. These could include:

- Large meetings where home churches can come together to share in the special gifting some strong teachers, preachers and evangelists offer.
- Missions-sending efforts which usually cost too much for any home church to fund on its own; ministry to the poor (home churches are usually weak or completely ineffective at developing meaningful community development ministries).
- Ministries to children and students (home churches tend to gravitate to a given age group and find it difficult to diversify into different age groups. Special thrusts to reach students are usually more effective when program-based. Even groups that started as student groups tend to "grow up" and lose their connection to student ministry).
- Counseling and support ministries that require more expertise than most home churches can deliver.
- Sharing expertise in a home church ministry (many home churches are very low on experience, so it makes sense to have some of the most experienced home church leaders available for consultation and advice. These usually have to be paid staff because the time demands of such availability would be too great for *tent makers*).
- Sharing theological expertise (theologians and scholars follow a special calling that is impractical for most home church leaders. It makes sense to arrange for clusters of home churches to share

access to theologically trained equippers who can take people's learning to the next level. By banning together, home churches can afford to have their own staff theologians and classes).

Index

Endnotes

Introduction

1. Quoted in Bob Fitts Sr., *Saturation Church Planting: Multiplying Congregations through House Churches*, self published, 1993, p. 12.

Chapter 1: Life in the Desert

1. North American population explosion is far outstripping church growth. Olson shows how that attendance in all American churches is projected to grow from 50 million in 1990 to 60 million in 2050. However, the population is projected to grow from 248 million in 1990 to 522 million during that same period.

2. Stuart Murray, *Church Planting: Laying Foundations* (Waterloo, Ontario: Herald Press, 2001), pp. 62-63.

3. Larry Kreider, *House Church Networks* (Ephrata, PA: House to House, 2001), p. 24.

4. Bob Roberts, Jr., *The Multiplying Church: The New Math for Starting New Churches* (Grand Rapids, MI: Zondervan, 2008), p. 65.

5. For more on this topic, read pp. 46–48 of *Natural Church Development* (Carol Stream, IL: ChurchSmart Resources, 1996).

6. Personal correspondence with Jamey Miller, pastor and founder of Christ Fellowship, a church planting movement-- www.ChristFellowship.org

7. As quoted in James Allen, "Why Plant a New Church?" Article accessed on Monday, January 03, 2005 from http://www.plantingministries.org/whyplant.htm.

Chapter 2: What is a Simple Church

1. Wolfgang Simson, *Houses that Change the World: The Return of House Churches* (Cumbria, UK: OM Publishing, 1998), p. xxi.

2. Westminster Confession of Faith, at http://www.pcanet.org/general/cof_chapxxi-xxv.htm#chapxxv.

3. The official definition of the Southern Baptist convention on June 14, 2000 and found at http://www.sbc.net/bfm. Scriptures included are: Matthew 16:15-19; 18:15-20; Acts 2:41-42,47; 5:11-14; 6:3-6; 13:1-3; 14:23,27; 15:1-30; 16:5; 20:28; Romans 1:7; 1 Corinthians 1:2; 3:16; 5:4-5; 7:17; 9:13-14; 12; Ephesians 1:22-23; 2:19-22; 3:8-11,21; 5:22-32; Philippians 1:1; Colossians 1:18; 1 Timothy 2:9-14; 3:1-15; 4:14; Hebrews 11:39-40; 1 Peter 5:1-4; Revelation 2-3; 21:2-3.

4. Richard R. DeRidder and Leonard J. Hofman, *Manual of Christian Reformed Church Government* (Grand Rapids, MI: Board of Publications of the Christian Reformed Church, 1994), p. 101.

5. Ibid.

6. Charles Brock, *Indigenous Church Planting: A Practical Journey* (Neosho, MO: Church Growth International, 1994), chapter 2 and chapter 4 as quoted in Ed Stetzer, *Planting New Churches in a Post-Modern Age* (Nashville, TN: Broadman and Holman Publishers, 2003), p. 171.

7. As quoted in Bob Fitts Sr., *Saturation Church Planting: Multiplying Congregations through House Churches,* self published, 1993, p. 8.

8. John Dawson, *Taking Your Cities for God* (Lake Mary, FL: Creation House, 1989).

9. Email posted to cellchurchtalk, 2/09/2006.

10. Men is not in the Greek text. The Easy to Read version (ERV) of this passage says: *Obey your leaders. Be willing to do what they say. They are responsible for your spiritual welfare, so they are always watching to protect you. Obey them so that their work will give them joy, not grief. It won't help you to make it hard for them.*

11. I believe that Christ's church should meet regularly together. I say this in opposition to the idea that a local church might simply be believers meeting "once in a while" at Starbucks or a Chris Tomlin concert. George Barna, in *Revolution* (Wheaton, Illinois: Tyndale House Publishers, 2005), pp. 144, says that a replacement "micro-model" might be: a worship conference, coaching communities, internet groups, parachurch ministries, . ." (66). He says, "Ultimately, we expect to see believers choosing from a proliferation of options, weaving together a set of favored alternatives into a unique tapestry that constitutes the personal 'church' of the individual" (66). He believes that the new "local church" of the revolutionaries might be in cyberspace, meeting with one's own family, or going to Chris Tomlin concerts.

12. Ephesians 5, Romans 14, and many other places say that any biblical church must be under Christ's Lordship.

Chapter 3: The First Simple Churches

1. "Pioneer Cell Church Planting, Part 4," (C&MA cell net newsletter, November 1999). Responses from Tim Westergren, Gordon Munro, and Raymond Ebbett. All quotes from Tim Westergren in this section are from the same source.

2. Personal email received from Tim on Tuesday, November 27, 2007.

3. David W. Shenk and Ervin R. Stutzman, *Creating Communities of the Kingdom: New Testament Models of Church Planting* (Scottdale, PA: Herald Press, 1988), pp. 94-95.

4. John Mallison, *Growing Christians in Small Groups* (London: Scripture Union, 1989), p. 5.

5. Roland Allen, *Missionary Methods: St. Paul's or Ours?* (Grand Rapid, MI: Eerdmans Publishing Co., 1962), p. 3. Roland Allen (1868 - 1947) was born in England. He was the son of an Anglican priest but was orphaned early in life. He trained for ministry at Oxford and became a priest in 1893. Allen spent two periods in northern China working for the Society for the Propagation of the Gospel. The first from 1895 to 1900 ended due to the Boxer Rebellion, during which Allen was forced to flee to the British legation in Beijing. He was chaplain to the community throughout much of the siege. After a period back in England,

he returned to north China in 1902, but was forced home due to illness. These "early experiences" led him to a radical reassessment of his own vocation and the theology and missionary methods of the Western churches. Allen became an early advocate of establishing churches which from the beginning would be self-supporting, self-propagating, and self-governing, adapted to local conditions, and not merely imitations of western Christianity. These views were confirmed by a trip to India in 1910 and by later research in Canada and East Africa. It is with this background that Allen wrote his book, *Missionary Methods,* which was first published in 1912. Allen's approach to mission strategy for indigenous churches is based on the study of Saint Paul's missionary methods, as he is convinced that in them the solution can be found to most of the difficulties of the day. He believed it was the recognition of the church as a local entity and trust in the Holy Spirit's indwelling within the converts and churches which was the mark of Paul's success. In contrast was Allen's belief that the people of his day were unable to entrust their converts to the Holy Spirit and instead relied in His work through them. Allens'views became increasingly influential, though Allen himself became disillusioned with the established churches. He spent the last years of his life in Kenya, establishing a reclusive church of his own devising, centered on an idiosyncratic "family rite."

6. Personal email received from church planter on Tuesday, April 08, 2008.

7. Bob Roberts, Jr., *The Multiplying Church: The New Math for Starting New Churches* (Grand Rapids, MI: Zondervan, 2008), p.87.

8. Email received on 4/15/2006 from Cellchurchtalk, an email chat list. The person who wrote this is Keith Bates, who is planting a church in Narrabri NSW, Australia.

9. Pastor Phil Crosson, cell church planter in Albany, Oregon, wrote to cellchurchtalk on Wednesday, September 13, 2000.

10. Ralph Moore, *Starting a New Church* (Ventura, CA: Regal Books, 2002), p. 37.

11. I like the Easy to Read version here (ERV). "What you have heard me teach publicly you should teach to others. Share these teachings with people you can trust. Then they will be able to teach others these same things."

12. Roland Allen, *Missionary Methods: St. Paul's or Ours?* (Grand Rapid, MI: Eerdmans Publishing Co., 1962), p. 93.

13. Brother Yun with Paul Hattaway, *The Heavenly Man* (Mill Hill, London: Monarch Books, 2004), p. 223.

Chapter 4: Do You Have What It Takes?

1. I've written two books on the gifts of the Spirit: *The Spirit Filled Small Group* (Grand Rapids, MI: Chosen Books, 2005) and *Discover* (Moreno Valley, CA: CCS Publishing, 2007). In both books I argue for what I call the "combination view" of the gifts of the Spirit. I believe that God has permanently given at least one gift to each believer (constitutional view), but that He often grants gifts according to the need at the time (situational view). Thus the "combination view" combines those two.

2. Aubrey Malphurs, *Planting Growing Churches* (Grand Rapids, MI: Baker Books,

1998), p. 108.

3. These particular church planters formed part of the Christian Church denomination. Aubrey Malphurs, *Planting Growing Churches* (Grand Rapids, MI: Baker Books, 1998), p. 103.

4. This quote is from an e-mail that Jim Egli sent to his statistical research professor at Regent University in spring 1997.

5. Email to cellchurchtalk, an internet chat site, on Saturday, November 24, 2001.

6. The cost to assess a church planter might range from $350 to $1000.00. The price includes an interview with an assessor that lasts between four to seven hours. Often the assessment is connected with a weekend training. Most insist on face to face interviews, but some assessors are willing to do the assessment via telephone. One assessor told me: "The cost to assess a church planter is approximately $450.00 (assuming the assessors are in the area and traveling great distances isn't required). That includes two assessors (a non-negotiable in this system) and about a four to seven hour interview followed up with a written report. The length of the interview depends greatly on the experience of the assessors and the depth of experience that the potential church planter brings to the table." Another assessor said to me, "I prefer to do it in tandem. This gives two voices, perspectives, experiences, and input when the practical application portions of the training takes place." Below are some recommended providers of in-depth assessments:

    *   Dr. Charles Ridley
        Indiana University, Bloomington, IN
        812-856-8340

    *   Dr. Peggy Mayfield
        Lawrenceville, GA
        770-995-1846

    *   Dr. Tom Graham
        LaHabra, CA
        562-697-6144

7. Ed Stetzer, *Planting New Churches in a Post-modern Age* (Nashville, TN: Broadman and Holman Publishers, 2003), p. 79.

8. Aubrey Malphurs, *Planting Growing Churches* (Grand Rapids, MI: Baker Books, 1998), p. 91.

Chapter 5: Root System 101

1. Norman Dowe on cellchurchtalk wrote these words on 3/19/2001.

2. Peter Wagner, *Church Planting for a Greater Harvest* (Ventura, CA: Regal Books, 1990), p. 44.

3. The first book, *Live,* starts the training by covering key Christian doctrines, including baptism and the Lord's supper. The second book, *Encounter* guides the believer to receive freedom from sinful bondages. The Encounter book can be used one-on-one or in a group. *Grow,* the third book, gives step-by-step instruction for having a daily quiet time, so that the believer will be able to feed him or herself through spending daily time with God. The fourth book,*Share,*

instructs the believer how to communicate the gospel message in a winsome, personal way. This book also has two chapters on small group evangelism. And then the fifth book, *Lead*, prepares the Christian on how to facilitate an effective cell group. This book also prepares someone to be part of a small group team. All of these books can be purchased at www.joelcomiskeygroup.com or by calling 1-888-344-CELL.

4. David W. Shenk and Ervin R. Stutzman, *Creating Communities of the Kingdom: New Testament Models of Church Planting* (Scottdale, PA: Herald Press, 1988), pp. 43-44.

5. *Elder* emphasizes spiritual maturity; *pastor* highlights the feeding and care role of the leader; *overseer* demonstrates the guardian role of the leader.

6. Audrey Malphurs, *Planting Growing Churches* (Grand Rapids, MI: Baker Books, 1998), p. 290.

7. You might be fortunate to have fulltime staff. At Wellspring, the staff meet each week to pray, nurture the small groups, and oversee the church. I like to start the staff meeting with a time of sharing from Scripture and prayer. Next is a time to review the progress of the small groups. In our weekly team meeting, for example, we each have a sheet of paper that tells us:

   - How many small groups we'd like to see at the end of the year (our goal)
   - A list of each cell with the attendance in the cell from the previous week
   - We then talk about each group, allowing team members to share what they know about the group, the leader, potential problems, and praise reports. In this way we truly pastor the church.
   - After discussing the life groups, we cover additional issues in the church, such as celebration service, various ministries, and calendar items. The weekly staff meeting usually last two hours. Like the root system, it provides nourishment for the rest of the tree.
   - If you don't have staff, do the same thing with your team of elders.

9. Peter Wagner, *Church Planting for a Greater Harvest* (Ventura, CA: Regal Books, 1990), p.72.

Chapter 6: Aiming Accurately

1. Accessed at http://www.openbiblecentral.org/models_church_planting.asp on Saturday, September 18, 2004.

2. Ralph Neighbour, email sent to cellchurchtalk on Wednesday, September 13, 2000.

3. Jeff doesn't personally touch alcohol. Yet he doesn't feel there's anything wrong with having a beer or glass of wine. He believes that the Bible speaks against drunkenness, not having a glass of wine.

4. The Frenches have tried some other approaches to meet people as well. Jeff joined the social committee of his housing association. He coached volleyball at the high school where his wife teaches. His wife, Laura, is equally involved. She has led the homecoming and prom committee at the local High School and helped with Habitat for Humanity youth build.

They both have worked with the local Boy's and Girls club, where Laura was able to use her Spanish to help those who are still learning English. Jeff was able to teach volleyball. Together they have been to the area Auburn Club, which networks Auburn University alumni (Jeff graduated from Auburn). The Frenches take advantage of their interest in college football by inviting people over to watch games and grill out. One last approach was to invite one couple over for dinner a week for a period of months. Some of these approaches were quite fruitful, while others were marginal at best. Jeff shared that they try things and see what happens. If it works, they keep up that approach. If not, they try to invest their time and energy somewhere else.

5. Phone conversation with Bill Mallick on Wednesday, January 05, 2005.

6. The 10-5-1 plan was posted by Rob Campbell on the Joel Comiskey Group blog on August 6, 2007 at 12:48 p.m. at www.joelcomiskeygroup.com.

7. Ralph Neighbour, *The Shepherd's Guidebook* (Houston, TX: Touch Publications, 1992), p. 86.

8. David Garrison, *Church Planting Movements: How God is Redeeming a Lost World* (Midlothian, VA: WIGTake Resources, 2004), p. 223.

9. David W. Shenk and Ervin R. Stutzman, *Creating Communities of the Kingdom: New Testament Models of Church Planting* (Scottdale, PA: Herald Press, 1988), p. 58.

10. David W. Shenk and Ervin R. Stutzman, *Creating Communities of the Kingdom: New Testament Models of Church Planting*, p. 62.

11. Personal email from Jeff Boerma on Friday, May 09, 2008.

Chapter 7: Simple Cell Church Planting

1. I'm not married to the word cell. My conviction is that we should be flexible about what name we use to describe our groups, while standing strongly behind the meaning or definition. As I travel worldwide, however, I find that most churches continue to use the word cell to describe their small groups. It's hard to escape the influence of David Cho, the modern day founder of the cell church movement. He coined the term cell to describe his groups back in the 70s and the worldwide cell church movement still uses this title. I do advise, however, not to use a name that emphasizes only one characteristic of the group. For example, fellowship groups, care groups, community groups, or even evangelism groups only describe one aspect of the group--thus the name itself can confuse people. I recommend choosing a name that grasps the full dynamic of the group (e.g., touch groups, life groups, heart groups, etc.).

2. David Hesselgrave, the author of more than twenty books, is professor emeritus of Trinity Evangelical Divinity School, Deerfield, Illinois. This article originally appeared in the January, 2000 issue of *Evangelical Missions Quarterly*.

3. As mentioned in an earlier endnote, I've developed my own training material. The first book, *Live*, starts the training by covering key Christian doctrines, including baptism and the Lord's supper. The second book, *Encounter* guides the believer to receive freedom from sinful bondages. The Encounter book can be used one-on-one or in a group. *Grow*, the third book, gives step-by-step instruction for having

a daily quiet time, so that the believer will be able to feed him or herself through spending daily time with God. The fourth book, *Share*, instructs the believer how to communicate the gospel message in a winsome, personal way. This book also has two chapters on small group evangelism. And then the fifth book, <u>Lead,</u> prepares the Christian on how to facilitate an effective cell group. This book also prepares someone to be part of a small group team. All of these books can be purchased at www.joelcomiskeygroup.com or by calling 1-888-344-CELL.

4. Many believe that cell churches are only large mega churches. David Garrison, expert on church planting movements, writes, "As with house churches, cell churches also tend to be homogenous in nature, but rarely embrace a vision to reach an entire people group. This is because the vision driving a cell church is to grow larger rather than to reach the entire people group or city through the church multiplication" (David Garrison, *Church Planting Movements: How God is Redeeming a Lost World*, Midlothian, VA: WIGTake Resources, 2004, p. 272)

5. Mega cell churches are certainly preferred to non-cell mega churches. The mega program-based church phenomenon is growing throughout North American, but the gravest problem, in my opinion, is that such churches subtly promote anonymity. I've also noticed that a majority of the attendees are from other churches. My estimate is that seven out of ten have migrated from a smaller church to attend the mega church. Why? Often it's the freedom that comes from non-accountability. Most people involved with mega churches admit that some congregations swell their ranks with the entertaining Sunday show. Gibbs says, "It must not be assumed that the impressive growth of many seeker-sensitive churches is due primarily to the conversion of the unchurched or to the reactivatation of the once-churched-but-subsequently-lapsed. The bulk of the growth is more likely through the transfer of church members, either because of relocation or because of disillusionment or boredom with their former church" (*Church Next*, Downer's Grove, IL: InterVarsity Press, 2000, p. 173). Some who study this phenomenon compare some mega churches with a giant chain store that comes into a town and puts all the little stores out of business. The smaller churches are often drained by the mega church down the street. It has created an unhealthy celebrity focus. Celebrities have been described as people well known for their well-knowness.

6. Personal e-mail sent to me in April 2002.

7. This wasn't always the case. Before starting the cell system in 1986, Elim had many church plants around the city, but then they decided to connect them together into a greater whole. Mario is thinking seriously about having satellite churches in various parts of the city in order to ease the driving load to the mother church.

8. The International Charismatic Mission in Bogota, Colombia is an example of the satellite approach. ICM established multiple satellite churches around Bogota which were connected to the mother church. Pastor César Castellanos meets with the pastors of each of these satellite churches during a Monday morning staff meeting. The satellite churches at ICM were established upon the cell groups that already existed in those outlying zones, thus maintaining the cell-based focus. Because many people do not have cars and the church is on the outskirts of the city, transportation is a major factor. The Elim Church in El Salvador deals with this problem by hiring over 600 buses to transport the 35,000+ people to the celebration services (there are three times this many in the cell groups). Cell groups themselves take offerings to charter these city buses. The buses wait at

church until the service is over and transport the people home again.

9.   When I visited the church in the year 2000, they had asked the satellite churches to attend the one large celebration service in the indoor stadium in Bogota, while still maintaining their distinct identity. After talking to several leaders and attending one of the satellite churches, I believe that it is correct to say that the church had approximately 11,000 attending the eleven satellite churches.

Chapter 8: How to Plant a Cell Church

1.   Bob Roberts, Jr., *The Multiplying Church: The New Math for Starting New Churches* (Grand Rapids, MI: Zondervan, 2008), p.66.

2.   Kitt Mason sent this information to cellchurchtalk on Wednesday, August 16, 2000. The information is adapted from an address given by Carol Davis at the World Impact Crowns of Beauty Conference, February 1999. Source: Dawn Ministries and *Joel-News-International*, 329, August 16, 2000.

3.   We gathered approximately 150 people who were willing to plant the church. We gathered those people in various planning meetings to prepare for the launch. I trained the small group leaders who were going to lead groups in the new church. On a particular Sunday in 1994, we held our first Sunday service.

4.   Jeannette Buller wrote this comment on 11/15/2001 to cellchurchtalk.

5.   Aubrey Malphurs, *Planting Growing Churches* (Grand Rapids, MI: Baker Books, 1998), p. 313.

6.   Peter Wagner, *Church Planting for a Greater Harvest* (Ventura, CA: Regal Books, 1990), p. 56.

7.   From the beginning this particular husband was more skeptical of cell church ministry, having been accustomed to the Sunday morning church experience for most of his upbringing. His wife was full of excitement and passion, and she was the reason for their involvement. Eventually they both left our church plant to find a more traditional church. And this is always the problem in finding "churched people" to be part of the pilot group. Often they are unwilling to wholeheartedly support a new vision, like cell church, because they are so accustomed to the way things were.

8.   Don Tillman wrote cellchurchtalk, an internet chat group on the cell church on Monday, May 15, 2000.

9.   For example, if someone is tired because of a busy week, that person would not skip Wellspring. Rather, he or she would not attend the other church in which he or she is celebrating. The other church is extra. In summary, any other church involvement is extra.

10.   Ralph wrote this to cellchurchtalk, an internet chat group on 5/11/2000.

11.   Don Tillman wrote cellchurchtalk, an internet chat group on the cell church on Monday, May 15, 2000.

12.   *Leadership Explosion* can be obtained at http://store.joelcomiskeygroup.com/leexmucegrto.html or by calling 1-888-344-CELL.

13.   A fulltime pastor could coach up to twelve cell leaders. This is an idea number and most likely it will be far less.

14. Rob sent the following email to me on July 25, 2002: "Our cells evangelize by building relationships with people outside the family of God—family, friends, co-workers, neighbors, school mates, etc. We build authentic relationships, love people, pray hard, and do 'teamwork' evangelism. I was struck one day by the pattern of evangelism in the New Testament--Jesus sends out the 12, 2x2. He sends out the 70, 2x2. You get to the book of Acts and it's Peter and John, Paul and Barnabas, Paul and Timothy, Paul and Luke, Paul and Silas (Paul and everybody), but it's always in teams. The only exception that I can think of is Philip ('The Evangelist'). Yet, we Americans do evangelism like we do everything else, in isolation, clinging to our individualism. So, we train, teach, and practice 'teamwork' evangelism. I build a relationship with my friend Jon. Jon likes golf, so I invite other members of my cell to play golf with my friend Jon. You've seen the church growth stuff about if someone doesn't make six friends within three months, they don't stick. Well, teamwork evangelism dramatically increases our chances of assimilation. Plus, many people are too timid to share their faith, but they are much bolder in teams. It works."

15. Jay Firebaugh, former senior pastor of Clearpoint Church in Pasadena, Texas, invented this order for multiplication. He offers the following additional insight: Don't expect the members in your cell to WANT to birth. In fact, if they wanted to get away from one another you would have a problem! These people have likely grown to value and love each other. They have longed for community in their lives and now a birth can seem a threat to losing it. Be empathetic! However, you have got to know that the greatest threat to community is becoming too large and / or ingrown. It is imperative that the Shepherd and Apprentice clearly believe and present that birthing is the best thing for the cell. If a cell doesn't birth at the appropriate time (around 15) one of two things will happen:

    • The group will continue to grow and become a medium-sized group rather than a cell. Community will be lost because sharing will become surfacy and safe. The small group dynamic will be lost and community will be lost along with it.

    • The group will stop growing and become ingrown. It will be "us four and no more!" When the focus moves away from the empty chair and evangelism and asking who else God would want to benefit from this group it is the beginning of the end! The group moves from the dynamic of "Christ in the midst" (Matthew 18:20) to navel-gazing.

    The only way to hold onto community is to let it go! Birthing allows the focus of the group to remain outward while continuing to encounter community within the dynamic of a cell. Be patient with your members as you take them through this process. Physical birth is difficult because the baby doesn't want to leave the safe environment of the womb for the unknown risk of the world outside their mother. But life is outside the womb! As you help your members through this traumatic time, you'll experience the life of God at work in and through your cell!

16. Bill Beckham, *Redefining Revival* (Houston, TX: Touch Publications, 2000), p. 216.

17. Bob Logan and Jeannette Buller, *Cell Church Planter's Guide* (Saint Charles, IL: ChurchSmart, 2001), 8-15.

18. In response to Jeffrey Long, Jason Hoag, wrote the above quote on cellchurchtalk www.cell-church.org on Tuesday, August 22, 2000.

19. Personal email sent to me on Friday, January 28, 2005.

20. Many churches do start with a celebration service. The Christian and Missionary Alliance launched 101 congregations in the United States and Puerto Rico on Sunday on April 19, 1987. The average attendance on that first Sunday was eighty-eight persons. Four years later, thirty-one churches were closed, thirty-four were under fifty people, twenty-four averaged between 50-100, and twelve churches were averaging over 100 people (Ken Davis, "A Hundred Churches in a Single Day," Doctoral Dissertation, Fuller Theological Seminary, January, 1992). I personally don't think this is a good average. I would also add that even through all church planting strategies have problems with transfer growth, it seems to me that the celebration strategy has the most difficulty. Why? Because anonymity is a key value. It's important not to ask for commitment right away. The goal is to allow the people to be anonymous. Neil Cole correctly asserts, "I went to a seminar on how to start a church. Church planting was reduced to simply getting more people in the seats on Sunday. Personally, I want to give my life to something bigger than that. In the seminar, the secret to growing a church was explained as revolving around two very important things: clean bathrooms and plenty of parking spaces. Apparently, the Kingdom of God is held up by dirty toilets and poor parking. Jesus will have to wait for us to clean up our act. In India and rural China, however, where the church is growing fastest, among the most noticeable missing ingredients are clean toilets and parking spaces, so I guess the theory espoused is not necessarily true" (Neil Cole, *Organic Church*, San Francisco, CA: Jossey-Bass, 2005, p. 94).

21. Lyle Schaller, *44 Questions for Church Planters* (Nashville, TN: Abingdon Press, 1991), p. 72.

22. As quoted in Peter Wagner, *Church Planting for a Greater Harvest* (Ventura, CA: Regal Books, 1990), p. 63.

23. Bob Logan recommends the following:
    - When there are three cells, celebration once per month
    - When there are five cells, celebration twice per month
    - When there are seven to eight cells, celebration every week.

    I like Logan's advice. I would simply tweak it to assure there are sufficient people in the seven to eight cells before starting the weekly celebration. Cells can be quite small (five to eight people), so even having seven to eight cells might mean there are only forty to fifty people. I do believe that a catalytic, gifted leader can start weekly celebrations with less people attending the cells. Eric Glover, the lead pastor of Wellspring, is sufficiently gifted to start celebration sooner than later.

24. 335 people showed up for the first service, and they estimated that between 180-200 were taking a look for the first time. Information gleaned from Coachnet: *The Cell Church Chronicles*, received on Monday, April 15, 2002 from Coachnet.

25. Personal e-mail Beckham sent to me on Sunday, May 19, 2002.

26. Lon Vining comments to cellchurchtalk on Monday, April 28, 2003.

27. The cell members at Elim normally gather in celebration gathering two to three times per week.

28. Ralph Moore, *Starting a New Church* (Ventura, CA: Regal Books, 2002), p. 117.

29. Peter Wagner, *Church Planting for a Greater Harvest* (Ventura, CA: Regal Books, 1990), pp. 120-121.

30. Bob Logan and Jeannette Bulller, *Cell Church Planters Guide* (Carol Stream, IL: ChurchSmart Resources, 2001). I heard this quote on this tape series.

Chapter 9: Planting House Churches

1. Check out the following references: Matthew 8:14-16; Luke 10:1-11; Acts 2:42-46, 10:1-48, 16:13-15, 16:29-34, 18:7-8, 20:5-12, 20:17-21, 28:30-31.

2. David Garrison, *Church Planting Movements: How God is Redeeming a Lost World* (Midlothian, VA: WIGTake Resources, 2004), p. 271.

3. Church history bears witness to the fact that whenever God has brought renewal, reform, and revival to the church and society, He has often sovereignly used house church and small group movements. A few examples are: the Priscillianists (4th century), the Monastics (4th century), the Waldenses (12th century), the Hussites (15th century), the Anabaptists (16th century), the Quakers (17th century), the Moravians (18th century), the Methodists (18th century), etc. [Taken from Rad Zdero, ed., *Nexus: The World House Church Movement Reader* (Pasadena, CA: William Carey Library, 2007), chs. 14, 18, and 19; Peter Bunton, *Cell Groups and House Churches: What History Teaches Us* (Ephrata, PA: House to House Publications, 2001)].

4. C. Kirk Hadaway, Start A. Wright, Francis M. DuBose, *Home Cell Groups and House Churches* (Nashville, TN: Broadman Press, 1987), p. 67.

5. There are some more recent examples of house church growth in non-restricted areas of the world. In the USA, for example, Neil Cole and Church Multiplication Associates have planted hundreds of organic churches that meet in homes, coffee shops, and just about anywhere. This network now has organic churches in thirty-six U.S. states and in thirty-one countries around the world (Neil Cole, "Case Study (USA): The Story of Church Multiplication Associates—From California to Chiang Mai in Seven Years," in *Nexus: The World House Church Movement Reader*, Rad Zdero, ed., [Pasadena, CA: William Carey Library, 2007], ch. 37). Similarly, in India, the world's largest democratic nation, Dr. Victor Choudhrie has given key apostolic leadership to seeing one hundred thousand house churches arise between the years 2001 and 2006 (Victor Choudhrie, "Case Study (India): How 100,000 House Churches were Started in Five Years," in *Nexus: The World House Church Movement Reader*, Rad Zdero, ed., (Pasadena, CA: William Carey Library, 2007), ch. 29).

6. Larry Kreider, *House Church Networks* (Ephrata, PA: House to House, 2001), p. 1.

7. Ed Stetzer, *Planting New Churches in a Post-modern Age* (Nashville, TN: Broadman and Holman Publishers, 2003), p. 172.

8. Bob Fitts, Sr. *Saturation Church Planting* (Riverside, CA: self-published, 1993), p. 30.

9. For more information on the organic church log onto http://www.cmaresources.org, For additional reading see: *Houses That Change the World* by Wolfgang Simson, *Cultivating a Life for God* by Neil Cole, *The Church Comes Home* by Robert and Julie Banks, *The Church Multiplication Guide* by George Patterson, *Missionary Methods: St. Paul's or Ours?* by Rolland Allen. Used by permission from *Organic Church Planters' Greenhouse Intensive Training Notes*, by Neil Cole and Paul Kaak, Church Multiplication Associates, 2001.

10. As quoted in Larry Kreider, *House Church Networks* (Ephrata, PA: House to House Publications, 2002) p. 12.

11. Neil Cole, *Organic Church* (San Francisco, CA: Jossey-Bass, 2005), p.xxvi.

12. Rad Zdero, "The Financial Support of House Church Leaders", in Nexus: The World House Church Movement Reader, Rad Zdero, ed., (Pasadena, CA: William Carey Library, 2007), ch.53.

13. Larry Kreider, *House Church Networks* (Ephrata, PA: House to House, 2001), p. 12.

14. Bob Fitts Sr., *Saturation Church Planting: Multiplying Congregations through House Churches,* self published, 1993, p. 3.

15. Larry Kreider, *House Church Networks* (Ephrata, PA: House to House, 2001), p. 41.

16. Rad Zdero, *The Global House Church Movement* (Pasadena, CA: William Carey Library, 2004), p. 113.

17. Rad Zdero, *The Global House Church Movement* , p. 105.

18. Larry Kreider and Floyd McClung, *Starting a House Church* (Ventura, CA: Regal Books, 2007), pp. 98-111.

19. Rad Zdero, ed., *Nexus: The World House Church Movement Reader* (Pasadena, CA: William Carey Library, 2007), chs.8, 9, 10, 13, and 50.

20. This quote entirely from Bill Beckham as he critiques the city-wide church concept of Wolfgang Simson (Bill Beckham, *Where Are We Now* (Houston, TX: Glocal Publications, 2005), pp. 166-169)

The New Testament church functioned in four primary ways:

The *basic cell community* unit that Jesus modeled with the twelve.

A *cluster or congregation* of basic cell units that Jesus modeled with the seventy and the one hundred twenty.

A *local church* referred to in the New Testament as "the whole church."

The *universal church* composed of all of Christ's local churches at all times of history.

In his house church hybrid model Wolfgang Simson believes in the universal expression of church as the large group expression. In this approach the church continues to be small independent groups of Christians meeting in houses in the classic "house church" expression of the church. The *new twist* is that the independent house church groups are encouraged to meet together from time to time in a "city church" expression as an "interdependent" expression of large group worship. This "city church" expression is supposed to take the place of the local large group expression of the church and to allow the local church to live as a simple "organic" house church.

This is a church that is strong in small group ministry and open to broad universal expressions of the church. But, it is weak in the area of a local church expression beyond a small group house church size. I think I understand why this approach has developed and why it has such strong appeal in certain groups within the church. The hybrid house church has a philosophical and maybe a historical connection to parachurch ministries.

The hybrid house church in the west developed as a reaction to two types of traditional churches. The state church in Europe is a dying large group church with little spiritual life. New Testament Christians in Europe have understandably been suspicious of large group expressions of the church. Many of these New Testament Christians have longed for an alternative and have been attracted to parachurch ministries and to small groups that are different from the state church model.

Simson's city church expression of the large group appeals to these two groups because it is totally different from the traditional local large group expression. This eliminates the need to deal with the large group expression of the church that has so miserably failed.

Therefore, it should not surprise us that Simson's hybrid house church model has no large group wing at the local church level. And, in its city expression, the large group is so far removed in distance, authority and common purpose that it severely weakens the life of the church at the implementing local church level. It is interesting that the house church movement outside of Europe and the United States generally develops a local large group expression of some sort. Think about China.

The use of a "city celebration" as a substitute for the large group wing is dangerous for house churches developing in both Europe and the United States. The problem with the hybrid house church model is that the large group and small group expressions of the church are not encouraged to come together as one integrated local body that is larger than the number of Christians that can crowd into a house.

The option for being church in the hybrid house church teaching of Simson is for a church to operate as a single cell unit in a "house church" expression and from time to time to meet in a large group expression as a "city church." This approach distorts the balanced nature of the New Testament church that flies with both a large group and small group wing.

This is the only way the church can experience and express the full nature of God as transcendent and immanent. The hybrid house church creates a bird with a strong small group wing. However, the large group wing of the hybrid house church only flaps when it gathers as a flock for "city celebration."

A local cell church can and should gather together in area "city celebration" with other churches when possible. This is beginning to happen in different cities around the world. "City celebration" is a way for local churches to experience the "universal" nature of the church in a practical venue while on earth. But, cell churches gather for these kinds of universal, city expressions as functioning two-winged churches.

They don't gather as one winged house groups looking for a large group expression so they can flap a large group wing. They do not substitute "city celebration" for local church large group expression.

In a cell church, "city celebration" is an addition to the local large group and it expresses the universal unity of the church in a powerful way. From a cell church perspective a "city celebration" is a group of two winged local churches that are flying in formation, going in the same direction, heading for the same destination and moving toward the same goal. They may get together for "city celebrations" from time to time. But all have fully functioning large and small group wings at the local church level. This city large group wing teaching must not be superimposed upon the other types of house churches such as in China.

And, these existing New Testament house church expressions must not be used to prove the validity of this flawed hybrid house church approach. What is happening in the house church movement in places such as China is not an example of the hybrid house church teaching on "city celebrations."

New Testament house churches will always have some kind of local large group expression. If independent house churches find it difficult to cooperate at a local church level, why do we think they will be effective in cooperating at a "city" church level? House churches need to practice large group life at the local level before expecting large group life to work at the universal city level.

21. Rad Zdero, *The Global House Church Movement* (Pasadena, CA: William Carey Library, 2004), pp. 108-109.

22. Rad Zdero, *The Global House Church Movement* , p. 106.

23. Larry Kreider, *House Church Networks* (Ephrata, PA: House to House Publications, 2002) p. 98.

24. Larry Kreider, *House Church Networks,* p. 63.

25. Bill Beckham, *Redefining Revival* (Houston, TX: Touch Publications, 2001), p. 170.

26. David Garrison, *Church Planting Movements* p. 193.

Chapter 10: Simple Reproduction

1. Charles Brock, *The Principles and Practices of Indigenous Church Planting* (Nashville, TN: Broadman Press, 1981), pp. 60-61.

2. David Garrison, *Church Planting Movements: How God is Redeeming a Lost World* Midlothian, VA: WIGTake Resources, 2004), p. 195.

3. Roland Allen, *The Spontaneous Expansion of the Church: and the Causes which Hinder It* (London: World Dominion Press, 1956), p. 17.

4. Stuart Murray, *Church Planting: Laying Foundations* (Waterloo, Ontario: Herald Press, 2001), p. 62.

5. Robert J. Vajko, "Why Do Some Churches Reproduce?" Evangelical Missions Quarterly (July 2005), pp. 294-299.

6. Jim Collins, *Good to Great and the Social Sectors* (Boulder, CO: Monograph, 2005), p. 34.

Appendix Two: Additional Options

1. Evangelical Free Church statement on church planting. Accessed on Monday, January 03, 2005 at http://pnwd.efca.org/planting.

2. Elmer Towns, *Getting a Church Started* (Lynchburg, VA: no publisher, 1982), p. 67.

3. Peter Wagner, *Church Planting for a Greater Harvest* (Ventura, CA: Regal Books, 1990), pp. 60-74.

Appendix Five: Bill Beckham and Celebration

1. The following is taken from Beckham's book *Where Are We Now?* (Houston, TX: Glocal Publications, 2005), pp. 156 - 169.

Printed in the United States
130141LV00001B/1/P

9 780979 067969